LUDWIG WITTGENSTEIN

HIS PLACE IN THE DEVELOPMENT OF SEMANTICS

FOUNDATIONS OF LANGUAGE

SUPPLEMENTARY SERIES

Editors

MORRIS HALLE, *MIT*

PETER HARTMANN, *Münster/W.*

K. KUNJUNNI RAJA, *Madras*

BENSON MATES, *Univ. of California*

J. F. STAAL, *Amsterdam*

PIETER A. VERBURG, *Groningen*

JOHN W. M. VERHAAR (Secretary), *Manila*

Ateneo de Manila University

VOLUME 3

THE HUMANITIES PRESS / NEW YORK

TULLIO DE MAURO

LUDWIG WITTGENSTEIN

HIS PLACE IN THE

DEVELOPMENT OF SEMANTICS

D. REIDEL PUBLISHING COMPANY / DORDRECHT - HOLLAND

SOLE DISTRIBUTORS FOR U.S.A. AND CANADA
THE HUMANITIES PRESS / NEW YORK

Library of Congress Catalog Card Number: 67–27175

Printed in The Netherlands by D. Reidel, Dordrecht

EDITORIAL NOTE

In recent research in semantics the attention of linguists has been deservedly concentrated on the works of Katz and Fodor, Katz and Postal, Katz, Bierwisch, Fillmore, Weinreich, Lyons and Staal. However, there is a distinctly different tradition of semantic studies, especially in Romance linguistics and some trends of continental European philosophy. This tradition has interesting affinities with the later Wittgenstein.

The present monograph pursues mainly those traditions, while leaving out of account, purely for reasons of delimitation of the subject matter, the more recent strands in semantic research. It was written three years ago, which is the reason why more recent studies, mainly as contained in Noam Chomsky's *Cartesian Linguistics*, which is of great importance for further research in the European tradition, has not been included. In his 'Prefatory Note' the author lists some later publications relating to certain issues brought up in this monograph.

The trend elaborated in the present monograph differs, perhaps, from recent research in semantics for the most part in that both the speech situation and those factors in speech resisting formalization by reason of their situational involvement receive considerably more attention in the former.

JOHN W. M. VERHAAR

V

36948

PREFATORY NOTE

Certain points of view adopted in this monograph have been elaborated and refined in later studies. As for the history of semantic theory, K. O. Apel brings out the importance of *Philosophical Investigations* ('Wittgenstein und das Problem des hermeneutischen Verstehens', *Zeitschrift für Theologie und Kirche* **63** (1966), 49–87) and N. Chomsky demonstrates the remarkable relevance of 17th- and 18th-century philosophy of language in *Cartesian Linguistics* (New York 1966); some further episodes in the history of rationalistic thought are discussed in my *Introduzione alla semantica* (Bari 1965; 2nd ed. 1966, pp. 47–72, 170–2); Saussure's position, here barely touched upon, is more closely examined in my introduction and commentary to the Italian translation of the *Cours de linguistique générale* (Bari 1967). The degree to which production and interpretation of the linguistic sign depend on the surrounding extra-linguistic framework has been studied by L. Prieto in *Principes de noologie* (The Hague 1964). My forthcoming paper 'Können wir die Bedeutung ausschalten?' (presented at the 'Tagung für Phonologie' held in Vienna in September 1966) again confirms the impossibility of describing phonemes or morphemes without reference to meaning. The concepts of 'meaning' and 'arbitrariness of meaning', techniques for describing meanings, and the notion of mutual dependence between semantic organization in a language and cultural organization in society are further elaborated in the *Introduzione alla semantica* cited above, as well as in two articles: 'Modelli semiologici: l'arbitrarietà semantica', *Lingua e stile* **1** (1966), 37–61, and 'Per una teoria del valore linguistico', *Lingua e stile* **2** (1967), 131–65.

TULLIO DE MAURO

TABLE OF CONTENTS

INTRODUCTION

Various students of general linguistics and semantics quote and discuss Wittgenstein, among others, OGDEN and RICHARDS (1960), ULLMANN (1951, 1962), PAGLIARO (1952, 1957), WELLS (1960), REGNÉLL (1960) and ZIFF (1960). For the most part however they quote the *Tractatus*[1] and not the *Philosophical Investigations*[2]; not all of them consider the most important ideas in the *Tractatus* but often discuss marginal points; above all they often make the discussion of Wittgenstein's ideas secondary to the development of their own thought. It should be added, moreover, that these students are exceptions. The large majority of language theorists, especially those with a philological background, have almost no knowledge of Wittgenstein's ideas. One scholar thinks that Wittgenstein's linguistic philosophy rests upon a grotesque misunderstanding of the workings of language (HERDAN, 1962, Chapter 24).

The present book seeks to draw the attention of students of general linguistics and semantics to the thought of both the early and the later Wittgenstein: not only the *Philosophical Investigations* but also the *Tractatus* is concerned with everyday language: Wittgenstein was thinking of the propositions of everyday language, when he affirmed that the proposition is a picture of reality (Chapter 1). This conception is very old, it is in fact found in Aristotle and it dominated ancient, mediaeval and modern rationalistic thought; only Locke, Vico and Leibniz criticized it strongly (Chapter 2). However, after the 18th century, the conception of language as a picture of reality flourished again in European culture and remained widespread: the responsibility is to be laid equally at the doors of Kant and of historical and scientific linguistics of the 19th and 20th centuries (Chapter 3). The early Wittgenstein started from a total acceptance of traditional ideas; but, by accepting these, he exposed all the consequences logically deriving from them up to the limits of absurdity; indeed – and here lies his historical merit – beyond absurdity. And in so doing he profoundly shook a conception which had lasted for centuries (Chapter 4). Linguistic solipsism, explicitly asserted by the early Wittgenstein, is implicit also in the early Croce's philosophy of language and in Saussure's general linguistics, that is in the thought of scholars who rejected traditional ideas of language (Chapter 5). The solipsistic conclusions of the early Wittgenstein, the early Croce, and Saussure seem to support those of contemporary semantic scepticism: but there are many reasons for rejecting this scepticism concerning the possibilities of communication or of semantics (Chapter 6). To the later Wittgenstein goes the merit of developing these reasons into a systematic conception. In the *Philosophical Investigations* Wittgenstein showed that it is not words which mean things but men who, by words, mean things, that a statement does not represent a fact, but that men, by a statement, mean facts: he also showed that by propositions men not only represent facts, but also live. Thus, the *Philosophical Investigations* are an adequate foundation for the construction of a new semantics as the science of signifying activity (Chapter 7).

NOTES

[1] The *Tractatus* is quoted here in the English translation by D.F. Pears & B.F. McGuinness (London 1961).
[2] *Investigations* are quoted here from the translation by G. E. M. Anscombe (Oxford 1958).

CHAPTER I

EVERYDAY LANGUAGE AS NOMENCLATURE
IN THE *TRACTATUS*

Not only the *Philosophical Investigations* but also of course the *Tractatus* of Wittgenstein is of great importance in the history of linguistic thought. This statement is not generally accepted, mainly for cultural reasons. Those most directly concerned with such a history are the students of general linguistics, but they seem to take little interest in Wittgenstein. The most recent works on the general history of linguistic thought (ARENS, 1955; LEROY, 1963; BOLELLI, 1965) do not quote Wittgenstein; indeed, they never even mention his name. Wittgenstein is mainly read by students of logic and of general philosophy; therefore the best-known aspects of his thought are those concerning logic and metaphysics or morals. Even Carnap (p. 261), writing as early as 1928, considered the two greatest merits of the *Tractatus* to be its contribution to logic and its ethical attitude. These two features have also drawn the attention of other scholars such as SCHOLZ (1962, p. 143), WEINBERG (1950, *passim*), COLOMBO (1959, *passim*), BARONE (1953, pp. 95–122). The latter speaks of the "linguistic solipsism" of Wittgenstein, but he stresses the noun and not the adjective. Everyone knows that there are linguistic theories in the early Wittgenstein, but these theories are usually presented as a bridge Wittgenstein built to get to logic and to an ethical attitude. There is, however, at least one notable exception to this rule. G. H. von Wright, Wittgenstein's successor at Cambridge, writes:

> "Wittgenstein's *Tractatus* may be called a synthesis of the theory of truth-functions and the idea that language is a picture of reality." (MALCOLM, 1958, p. 8).

This scholar therefore clearly recognizes that linguistic theories play an essential part in the structure of the *Tractatus*.

There is perhaps a second reason why this fact is not generally recognized. Discussing Wittgenstein and Weinberg, PAGLIARO (1952, p. 309) states:

> "The notion of an elementary proposition, whose noun is a proper noun,

that is, identical with the object it designates, is not that of a linguistic proposition. The language with which mathematical logicians are concerned is not really our language, that is, pure phonic language [...]".[1]

And similarly BARONE (1953, p. 103):

"An important aspect of Wittgenstein's doctrine should be clear: linguistic symbolism is studied in the form of a projective representation of reality; any evocative overtone of language, its normative function, its capacity to create worlds different from the world of cognition, is ignored or neglected. Language is considered only as an instrument of cognition; so long as this is kept in mind, it becomes perfectly understandable that neo-positivist thinkers should find in Wittgenstein a model and an approach for the analysis of scientific language."[2]

The thesis of these two distinguished scholars may perhaps be summarized as follows: when Wittgenstein looks at language he emphasizes its logical aspects. Only an imperceptible step separates this idea from the belief that Wittgenstein was not interested in everyday language, but in the symbolic and artificial language of logic. Whoever combines this belief with an interest in everyday language will clearly tend to neglect Wittgenstein and to believe that Wittgenstein's thought is not relevant to the problems in which he is interested. There is, however, no justification for this misapprehension. It is true that, when the early Wittgenstein looked at language, he mainly saw what we may call its "logical aspects". (Perhaps, later this will be the opinion of Wittgenstein himself: *Investigations* 3.) But it is also true that he was looking not at the language of logic, but at everyday language, and that his statements about language were intended to refer to all language, to every proposition (see also ANSCOMBE, 1959, pp. 25ff, 87–97).

There are two ways of showing that the *Tractatus* is concerned not with the language of logic and with logical propositions alone, but with the whole of language and every proposition. First by examining a series of statements from the *Tractatus* itself.

"We use the perceptible sign of a proposition (spoken or written etc.) as a projection of a possible situation. The method of projection is to think out the sense of the proposition." (3.11)

The inclusion of spoken propositions already confirms that Wittgenstein was thinking about everyday propositions. So one and the same sign (written or spoken etc.) can be common to the two different symbols – in which case they will signify in different ways.

4

Here also it is clear – aside from the customary reference to the spoken word – that Wittgenstein is thinking of the signs of current language, equivocal and not univocal as they would be in a formalized language, in, that is "a sign-language that is governed by *logical* grammar – by logical syntax" (3.325) (italics Wittgenstein's).

"In everyday language it very frequently happens that the same word has different modes of signification, and so belongs to different symbols – or two words that have different modes of signification are employed in propositions in what is superficially the same way. Thus the word 'is' figures as the copula, as a sign for identity, and as an expression for existence; 'exist' figures as an intransitive verb like 'go', and *identical* as an adjective; we speak of *something*, but also of *something's* happening.

(In the proposition 'Green is green' – where the first word is the proper name of a person and the last an adjective – these words do not merely have different meanings: they are *different symbols*.)" (3.323)

Any comment here is superfluous, as it is also in relation to the following passages from the *Tractatus*:

"Man possesses the ability to construct languages capable of expressing every sense, without having any idea how each has meaning or what its meaning is – just as people speak without knowing how the individual sounds are produced.

Everyday language is a part of the human organism and is no less complicated than it.

It is not humanly possible to gather immediately from it what the logic of language is."

"The tacit conventions on which the understanding of everyday language depends are enormously complicated." (4.002)

"When translating one language into another, we do not proceed by translating each *proposition* of the one into a *proposition* of the other, but merely by translating the constituents of propositions." (4.025)

"In fact all the propositions of our everyday language, just as they stand, are in perfect logical order." (5.5563)

It is clear from these examples, and from others which could be quoted, that in the *Tractatus* Wittgenstein was already seeking to make statements about the nature of language, of propositions, and of linguistic signs in general. (Whether these statements really comprehend *all* the characteristics of language in general is, of course, a different matter.)

A second way of showing that Wittgenstein was looking at the whole of language and at everyday propositions is offered by von Wright's short biography.

"The oldest parts of the *Tractatus* are those dealing with logic. Wittgenstein had formed his principal thoughts on these matters before the outbreak of the war in 1914, and thus before his twenty-sixth year. Later he became engrossed in a new problem. It was the question of the nature of the significant proposition. Wittgenstein told me how the idea of language as a *picture* of reality occurred to him. He was in a trench on the East front, reading a magazine in which there was a schematic picture depicting the possible sequence of events in an automobile accident. The picture there served as a proposition; that is, as a description of a possible state of affairs. It had this function owing to a correspondence between the parts of the picture and the things in reality. It now occurred to Wittgenstein that one might reverse the analogy and say that a *proposition* serves as a *picture*, by virtue of a similar correspondence between *its* parts and the world. The way in which the parts of the proposition are combined – *the structure* of the proposition – depicts a possible combination of elements in reality, a possible state of affairs." (MALCOLM, 1958, pp. 7–8)

It is clear from this biographical detail that, when he affirmed that propositions are pictures of reality, Wittgenstein was in fact thinking of the propositions of everyday language.

Wittgenstein, then, wanted to study everyday language. This raises the question whether those who study everyday language should study Wittgenstein. The question is certainly legitimate. Actually, Wittgenstein's main idea, that a proposition is a picture of reality, concerns everyday language, but that is no more than a platitude. It is on a par with the conception of language which MARTINET (1960, pp. 14–15) recently criticized:

"According to a very naïve, but quite widespread idea, a language is a repertory of words, that is of vocal (or written) signs, each one of which corresponds to one thing: that particular repertory known as the French language supposedly establishes a correspondence between a certain determinate sound graphically represented as *cheval* and a certain animal, the horse; differences between languages are thus reduced to differences in designation: for *cheval* the English say *horse* and the German *Pferd*; learning a second language would on that view simply consist in memorizing a new nomenclature similar to the old at every point. The few cases where you are forced to note exceptions to this parallelism are then called 'idioms' [...]. This idea of the language-repertory is based upon the simplicistic notion that the whole world is ordered, previous to man's vision of it, into categories of objects, all of which are perfectly distinct from each other, and each of which is necessarily identified by a name in each language."[3]

6

There is no doubt that Wittgenstein has this same "very naïve" conception of language which Martinet (and before him SAUSSURE, 1922, pp. 34, 97, 158) so effectively criticizes. If we wish fully to understand the grandeur of the historical contribution of Wittgenstein's thought we must, paradoxical though it may seem, trace the history of this time-honoured conception to demonstrate adequately its banality.

NOTES

[1] A. PAGLIARO (1952, p. 309): "La nozione di proposizione elementare, i cui nomi sono dei nomi propri, cioè identici con l'oggetto che designano, non è di proposizione linguistica. Il linguaggio di cui parlano i logici matematici, non è veramente il nostro linguaggio, cioè il puro linguaggio fonico [...]."

[2] BARONE (1953, p. 103): "Si precisa un aspetto di grande rilievo nella dottrina di Wittgenstein: il simbolismo linguistico viene studiato nella sua forma di rappresentazione proiettiva della realtà; ogni suggestione evocativa del linguaggio, la sua funzione normativa, la capacità di costituzione di sfere diverse dalla conoscitiva, sono ignorate o trascurate. Il linguaggio è considerato esclusivamente strumento di conoscenza; sotto questo aspetto è del tutto comprensibile come i pensatori neopositivisti trovino un modello e un suggerimento per l'analisi del linguaggio scientifico nell'analisi di Wittgenstein."

[3] MARTINET (1960, pp. 14–15): "Selon une conception fort naïve, mai assez répandue, une langue serait un répertoire de mots, c'est-à-dire de productions vocales (ou graphiques), chacune correspondant à une chose: à un certain animal, le cheval, le répertoire particulier connu sous le nom de langue française ferait correspondre une production vocal déterminée que l'ortographe représente sous la forme *cheval*; les différences entre les langues se ramèneraient à des différences de désignation: pour le cheval, l'anglais dirait *horse* et l'allemand *Pferd*; apprendre une seconde langue consisterait simplement à retenir une nouvelle nomenclature en tous points parallèle à l'ancienne. Les quelques cas où il faut bien constater des entorses à ces parallélisme constitueraient des 'idiotismes' [...] Cette notion de langue-répertoire se fonde sur l'idée simpliste que le monde tout entier s'ordonne, antérieurment à la vision qu'en ont les hommes, en catégories d'objets parfaitement distinctes, chacune recevant nécessairement une désignation dans chaque langue [...]."

CHAPTER II

LANGUAGE AS NOMENCLATURE FROM
ARISTOTLE TO LEIBNIZ' CRITICISM

The first systematic analysis of the conception of language as a repertory is very old. It is in fact found in Aristotle, and in embryo already in the fragments of Democritus. Consider the opening of the brief, but fundamental essay *On Interpretation* (16 a 3ff):

> "The things of the voice are symbols of the things of the spirit, and the writings are symbols of the things of the voice. And as the alphabet is not the same for everybody, neither are voices, though the former are always the basic signs of the latter. States of mind are the same for everyone, as are things, and these states are the reflections of things which are the same for everyone." [1]

It is very probable that the conception Aristotle expressed in these lines sprang from the convergence of two different lines of thought. On the one hand there was the need to reach a phenomenological description of linguistic facts more precise and systematic than the one which had previously existed. On the other hand there was the need to find, in the fact that each word has a meaning "which is the same for everyone", a basic guarantee of the principle of identity; that is, a guarantee such that not even he who denies the existence of the identity principle could disregard it. The latter line of thought has been well analysed by SCARAVELLI (1942, pp. 5–7ff). This subject, together with that of the structure of Aristotle's linguistic thought, must be discussed elsewhere: here we only wish to indicate its logical and historical consequences.

The meaning of Aristotle's position is clear. As graphic forms, beyond the differences in writing and alphabet, should and do faithfully reflect the forms of spoken language, so the latter, beyond purely extrinsic variations, must reflect our perceptions of reality with equal exactitude, perceptions which in their turn are no more than the reflections of the organization of reality in genera, species, and individuals.

For centuries interest in language was suffocated by the survival of Aristotle's ideas. To Aristotle, language is not a force actively intervening in the life of man, but just the transcription of sequences of concepts. It is important to learn to speak a language, as it is important to learn to write. But, a science of writing would teach us very little about the life of man, and that would be true also of a science of language concerned along the same lines. Any interest in language arising in the framework of Aristotelian ideas is bound to be a purely practical and normative, not an independent and scientific one. Each word is a door to the castle of universal concepts: we must of course be able to open the doors, but it is getting into the castle that is important. Such a conception could, and did, give birth to a normative grammar, not to a science of linguistics. Scientific linguistics only came to birth when Aristotle's ideas began to be challenged. We must reveal two implications of the Aristotelian conception if we are to understand when and how this came about.

If Aristotle's ideas had been correct, the analysis of a language could and should have been, from a heuristic point of view, the best source for a complete knowledge of reality; the use of language, moreover, would imply such a complete knowledge in those speaking it. In fact these two implications did not remain simple logical corollaries, but influenced the cultural organization of the late classical and mediaeval world. The former implication fathered the verbalism dominating later classic and mediaeval science (LENOBLE, 1957, pp. 382–389). The manifesto of verbalism was written by the bishop Isidorus (*Etymol.* I, 7, 1 L.):

> "The name (*nomen*) is so called as a notation (*notamen*), since its sound makes the things known (*notae*) to us. Unless you know the name, the knowledge of the thing itself disappears." [2]

The second was responsible for the chaining of grammatical descriptions to theories of formal logic. The grammarians wrote, as Vico later observed, as if people discovering languages "first had to go and sit at Aristotle's feet, by whose principles [the grammarians] had thought". [3]

The crisis of the Aristotelian conception arose when these two features of it began to be questioned. The advent of experimental science and the methods of classification of the natural sciences demonstrated, from the seventeenth century on, that there existed things which could be scientifically known and could be set in a chain of cause and effect relationships or placed in an organized relationship of genus, species and family, without ever having had a name in any language (but having a name in the "mathematical language": GALILEI, *Opere*, VI, p. 232). At the same time when the development of experimental and descriptive science took place, it became progressively clearer that the lexicon of a language was neither the only nor the best source for the scientific knowledge of reality, as Isidorus had believed (GUYÉNOT, 1957, pp. 25, 94–104; PRETI, 1950, p. 79; ROSSI, 1957, pp. 408–12; ROSSI, 1962, pp. 16–74; SPINK, 1960, pp. 59, 69, 125, 247, 266; VIANO, 1960, pp. 471–72).

The Renaissance witnessed growing interest in the comparison of languages. These comparative approaches gave rise to the idea that each language had its own "genius". Every language is different from others not so much because of the extrinsic difference of sounds, but because every language has a vocabulary and a syntax which do not coincide with those of other languages. In other words, what Martinet calls the "entorses", the distortions, of linguistic parallelism and what Vico calls "the almost infinite details which anyone who wants to argue about a language naturally encouters" [4] come into the foreground.

This patrimony of scattered observations bears fruit in the work of four great thinkers who make it the theme of systematic reflection. Francis BACON (1665, coll. 144–47) observes that every language has its own way of organizing meanings: there are Latin words which have no equivalent in Greek, and Hebrew words which have no equivalent in either Latin or Greek. And these are not isolated words alone: entire sections of the vocabulary are organized in different ways in different languages. Differences in language are without doubt to be explained, according to Bacon, by the differing characters of the peoples who use them.

John Locke (*An Essay Concerning Human Understanding*, III, V, §§ 7–16) moves along the same lines: he stresses the role entailed by the learning and use of nouns for the development of ideas. The latter, therefore, are not innate, but intimately linked to the various histories, and in particular to the various languages, of individual communities. Locke develops his analysis to the point of questioning, with telling examples, the possibility of translating phrases of one language into phrases of another. He emphasizes that beyond the school-established equivalents between Latin and English vocabularies, Latin and English words in actual fact evoke profoundly different worlds of culture and ideas. The relations between words and things are problematic and it is not possible to have a science of things founded only on words (CASSIRER, 1954, vol. I. p. 73ff; VIANO, 1960, pp. 469–76). There are those who characterize these ideas as "Humboldtian" (MOUNIN, 1963, *passim*): but they were already well-known in the seventeenth century and were fully worked out in Germany and in the Kingdom of Naples in the early years of the eighteenth century

The whole third book of Leibniz' *Nouveaux essays sur l'entendement humain* (LEIBNIZ, 1860, pp. 296–335) is dedicated to problems of linguistic philosophy. Every language, Leibniz explains, steers its own course to maintain the necessary balance in its vocabulary between widely-used general terms, with broad and generic meanings, and special terms, less often adopted and with definite and particular meanings. Leibniz also demonstrates, with an abundance of examples, the lack of coincidence or parallels in syntactic constructions and grammatical systems. As a consequence, every language has its own particular topography, not only on the phonic level but also on the semantic one. No language is merely the phonic clothing of a body of universal concepts and categories: on the contrary, each has the power to mould the thought of the communities adopting it.

From the other end of Europe Vico now picks up the burden of the Locke and Leibniz' theme. This scholar has been misunderstood even in recent times, his name being commonly associated with that of Croce and with the thesis of the identity of language and aesthetic activity (CALOGERO, 1947, pp. 105, 175). Pagliaro was the first to protest against this unjustified association (PAGLIARO, 1952, p. 47). He later sought to put Vico in his true light in a lengthy analytical study (PAGLIARO, 1961, p. 298–364). Vico is usually pictured as a scholar who had certain ideas about history from which, *as a consequence*, he derived certain ideas about language. The thesis of the poetic nature of language is considered to be at the centre of these ideas. LEROY (1963, pp. 12–13) presents a clear example of this manner of interpreting Vico, but unjustly so: Vico himself in his *Scienza nuova* (§§ 34, ed. Nicolini) stated that the keystone of this thought, acquired at the price of "the unyielding research of all *his* life as a scholar", is his conception of language. In his opinion, the history of language as he conceived it, is the cornerstone of the history of ideas, of religion, of jurisprudence (§§ 34, 35, 145, 161). Contrary to prevailing opinion, Vico (as he himself declared and as Pagliaro demonstrates) has certain ideas about language and, *as a consequence*, sees the history of nations in a certain way.

After Pagliaro's essay, it is possible to state briefly Vico's ideas on language. He in no way maintains the identity of intuition and expression, of speech and aesthetic activity; not only does he lack the concept and intention but the words themselves for such an end. He argues instead that it is a mistake to see in languages the reflections of the universal categories and concepts dear to Aristotelians and rationalists, categories

11

and concepts pre-existing to any activity of man. This conception Vico beleived, as the avant-garde of general linguistics still believes, to be "very naïve". We have already noted his arguments on the matter. Languages are older than Aristotle. They express a knowledge which is not of a rational kind, language's way of associating things and of classifying them by their names is a fantastic and a poetical way, not a rational and philosophical one. We should affirm, with Vico, that language cannot be brought under the common denominator of one single universal type of logic; each language forms its own patterns during the organization of human experience into meanings. And even when languages begin to express a common rationality their traditional basis persists and survives. French and Latin, Greek and the Germanic languages have each a different "genius" stemming from differing national characteristics (§§ 151, 152, 158, 159, 445, 530, 773, 994).

The closing years of the seventeenth century and the opening ones of the eighteenth were thus a decisive turning-point in the history of linguistic thought. For the first time it became absolutely clear that languages are not transcriptions of universally equal and predefined concepts, but rather the historically diversified bases upon which notions and concepts are built (which in their turn also differ from one period and country to another). It is thus possible to look with renewed interest at the historical diversification of languages. Vico dedicates a large part of his thought and writings to characterizing the typology of the various languages with which he was acquainted. He remains, however, practically alone in Italian culture.

Leibniz' fate was different. Like Vico, he dedicated a large part of his encyclopaedic enquiries to perfecting his knowledge of the typology and genealogy of the various European languages. But, unlike Vico, Leibniz was, in his time, a man of great influence on German and European culture. He was able to organize and set in motion the first concrete linguistic research, while Vico's project for a "mental dictionary" of the ideas common to various communicating languages remained an isolated effort (APEL, 1963, pp. 307ff, 371ff).

There is no doubt that the ideas, maturing from the late Renaissance onwards and systematized in the writings of Vico, Bacon, Locke and Leibniz, created a favourable atmosphere for the development of historical research on languages. It is important to note that such analyses were initially focussed above all on what, with Martinet, we may call the "first articulation" of linguistic signs and systems. They concerned, that is,

12

meaning and organizational peculiarities of meanings in various languages with attention to syntactical functions and peculiarities. It was an interest in the semantic and syntactic history of languages that produced the embryonic linguistics of Locke, Leibniz and Vico, and the studies of Hamann, Herder, Fr. and A. Schlegel and W. von Humboldt. Any interest in a "second articulation", in phonemes and in the phonematic consistency of words is almost entirely absent. Re-elaborated in the German and European cultural tradition of Hamann, Herder, Fr. Schlegel and W. von Humboldt, these ideas have accompanied and justified the establishment of a specialized technique of linguistic analysis, and the rise of the science of linguistics.

Histories of scientific linguistics barely register these facts. (Here also Apel's *Idee der Sprache* is an exception.) After some reference to the Greeks and Indians, they begin, not with Francis Bacon, Locke, Leibniz or Vico, but with Franz Bopp (SAUSSURE, 1922, p. 14; MEILLET, 1937, p. 457; BELARDI, 1959, p. 51; LEROY, 1963, pp. 17–21 etc.). Meillet, though giving credit to Humboldt for having been instrumental in Bopp's nomination in the University of Berlin, finds the former's ideas inadequate, and really no more than "the creation of an historical aspiration" (MEILLET, 1937, p. 460). LEROY (1963) devotes several pages to Humboldt, but only after he has made it clear that "it was the concept of the kinship of languages which set linguistics on a rational path" and explained that "it was only with Franz Bopp that certain proofs of the kinship of the Indo-European languages were established".

Protests against this way of presenting the beginnings of the science of linguistics have not been lacking. TESNIÈRE (1959, p. 13) for example writes:

"While modern linguistics exalts Bopp, the father of comparative grammar, to the heavens, it does far less than full justice to Wilhelm von Humboldt, who was a linguist of the highest order and gifted with the inspirations of a genius. That Meillet considered this ranking of linguists justified is, to say the least of it, paradoxical if the commonly accepted relative importance of these two scholars is taken into account. Historians of ideas, on the other hand, have not been deceived in this respect and do not hesitate to recognize in Humboldt a mind vastly superior to that of Bopp, who never surpassed the level of a good technical specialist, in Humboldt, the friend of Schiller and of Goethe. Those with some knowledge of the evolution of German thought in the nineteenth century would be justifiably surprised to learn that linguists have seen nothing strange in setting Humboldt, with his universal and highly cultivated mind, endowed in particular with a profound scientific knowledge, lower in the scale of values, be it of linguistic values, than a

13

simple comparative grammarian like Bopp [...]. Linguistics will inevitably one day be led to do full justice to Humboldt [...]." [5]

Tesnière perfectly grasped the absurdity of beginning the history of scientific linguistic studies with Bopp, and recognized that not only a problem of historical erudition but also a complex theoretical issue was involved. Hence his passion in defending Humboldt against Bopp, as a "universal and highly cultivated spirit" with a "profound scientific knowledge". This notwithstanding, Tesnière did not succeed in looking beyond Humboldt, in going further backwards in time. Tesnière was acutely aware of the problem of the historical origins and theoretical background of linguistics: he offers the best proof of the profound gulf separating seventeenth century linguistic thought from the linguistics of the late eighteenth and nineteenth centuries.

It is here indispensable to understand the why and how of this gulf if Wittgenstein's thought is to be completely understood. And a semantics secure from radical criticism can only be constructed if the reasons that create this gulf, and, therefore, Wittgenstein's thought are understood: *nihil sine doctrina miracula.*

NOTES

[1] Aristot., *De int.*, 16 a 3 ff.: "Ἔστι μὲν οὖν τὰ ἐν τῇ φωνῇ τῶν ἐν τῇ ψυχῇ καθημάτων σύμβολα, καὶ τὰ γραφόμενα τῶν ἐν τῇ φωνῇ. καὶ ὥσπερ οὐδὲ γράμματα πᾶσι τὰ αὐτά, οὐδὲ φωναὶ αἱ αὐταί. ὧν μέντοι ταῦτα σημεῖα πρῶτον, ταὐτὰ πᾶσι παθήματα τῆς ψυχῆς, καὶ ὧν ταῦτα ὁμοιώματα πράγματα ἤδη ταὐτά."

[2] "Nomen dictum quasi notamen, quod nobis vocabulo suo res notas efficiat. Nisi enim nomen scieris, cognitio rerum perit."

[3] "[Le quali cose tutte sembrano più ragionevoli di quello che Giulio Cesare Scaligero e Francesco Sanzio ne han detto a proposito della lingua latina. Come se i popoli che si ritruovaron le lingue] avessero prima dovuto andare a scuola d'Aristotile, coi cui princìpi ne hanno amendue ragionato!"

[4] G. B. Vico, 'Idea d'una grammatica filosofica', in G. B. Vico, *Opere*, a cura di Fausto Nicolini (Milano-Napoli 1953), pp. 944–45, p. 944: "[Giulio Cesare della Scala, seguitato poi da tutti i migliori grammatici che gli vennero dietro, si diede a ragionare delle cagioni della lingua latina co' princìpi di logica. Ma in ciò gli venne fallito il gran disegno, con attaccarsi a' princìpi di logica che ne pensò un particolare uomo filosofo, cioè con la logica di Aristotele, i cui princìpi, essendo troppo universali, non riescono a spiegare] i quasi infiniti particolari che per natura vengono innanzi a chiunque vuol ragionare di una lingua."

[5] "Guillaume de Humboldt [...] linguiste de grande classe, aux intuitions de génie, auquel la linguistique moderne est loin de rendre pleine justice, alors qu'elle porte aux nues Bopp, le père de la grammaire comparée. Meillet estimait que cette échelle des valeurs des linguistes était justifiée, ce qui est au moins paradoxal, si l'on songe à l'importance relative reconnue à ces deux esprits. Les historiens des idées, eux, ne s'y sont pas trompés, et n'hésitent pas à voir dans Humboldt, ami de Schiller et de Goethe,

un esprit très supérieur à Bopp, qui n'a jamais depassé le niveau d'un bon technicien spécialisé. Ceux qui ont quelque notion de l'évolution de la pensée allemande au XIXe siècle s'étonneront à bon droit que les linguistes n'aient pas été sensibles à ce qu'il y a d'étrange à classer dans l'échelle des valeurs, fût-ce des valeurs linguistiques, un esprit universel hautement cultivé et armé en particulier d'une culture scientifique approfondie, comme Humboldt, après un simple technicien de la grammaire comparée comme Bopp, [...] La linguistique sera fatalement amenée à rendre un jour pleine justice à Humboldt [...]."

CHAPTER III

ARISTOTELIC AND RATIONALISTIC SURVIVALS
IN HISTORICAL LINGUISTICS

"I do not explain here many other nouns, which I have already used, or I will use later, because they seem to me clear in themselves. And I have often noticed that philosophers err by trying to explain by logical definitions what is elementary and clear in itself, making it in that way more obscure. And when I said that the proposition *I think, therefore I am* is the first and most certain statement [...], I did not deny that it is previously necessary to know what *thought, existence, certainty*, mean; but, because these are elementary notions [...], I thought that it was not necessary to enumerate them." [1]

Descartes wrote these words several generations before Locke, Leibniz and Vico. Accepting here, as elsewhere in his work, Aristotelic and scholastic viewpoints, Descartes affirms that words are absolutely transparent means of expressing thought. Being such, they do not deserve any particular attention because they cannot alter conditions of doubt or certainty. The Aristotelic opinion was thus clothed, in seventeenth-century France, with the new authority of Descartes, and the *Grammaire générale et raisonné de Port Royal*, in which the thesis of the punctual adherence of linguistic forms and categories to concepts and categories of a universal order was analytically developed, was thus at once of Aristotelian and of Cartesian inspiration (ARENS, 1955, p. 72ff).

Our problem is to understand how this conception, apparently discredited by Locke, Leibniz and Vico, by the pre-romantic German thinkers and by W. von Humboldt re-flowered in European culture and remained "*assez répandue*", "very widespread". The responsibility (if so it may be called) for this is to be laid equally at the doors of Kant and of the historical and scientific type of linguistics prevalent in the nineteenth and twentieth centuries.

Kant's position in the history of linguistic thought is very peculiar. It is obvious for the average reader that Kant did not work on language. None the less the philosophical circles in which Kant's ideas were formed were saturated with discussions on language. This fact however is not taken into consideration even by the most comprehensive histories of philosophy.

It is well-known that the years around 1769 marked a decisive turning point in the development of Kant's thought. There is no doubt that this development was connected with Kant's reading of Leibniz' *Nouveaux Essays*, which were first published in 1765, though written at the beginning of the century. The book undoubtedly brought Kant to reconsider Locke's *Essay* and the works of the English empirical tradition (TONELLI, 1955, §§ 149–64; 1964, p. 234). We have already discussed the part that reflections on language play in Locke and Leibniz. It is worth noting that in the later English philosophers, Berkeley and Hume, this part grows in importance (see HUME, 1739, p. 38). It is moreover important, for what we shall say later, to emphasize that the *Metakritik* written by Kant's friend Johann Georg Hamann opens by quoting this page. The turning point in Kant's thought, and his re-awakening from his "dogmatic slumber" were therefore consequences of books in which new philosophical ideas appeared coupled to new ideas on language and meaning. Hamann, moreover, lived in the same city and frequented the same circles as Kant; the two corresponded, made plans to collaborate, argued. It was the issues raised by language which led to estrangement between Hamann and Kant. Both in the *Metakritik* (J. G. HAMANN, 1955, pp. 281–89) and in many of his notes, Hamann stresses the fact that reason, the apriori, the Cartesian *propositiones primae ac certissimae,* presuppose something else: language. And he writes (*Metakritik*, p. 268):

"Thus no deduction is necessary to show that language is the original ancestor in the genealogy of the seven sacred functions of logical premises and conclusions. Not only is the entire possibility of thinking founded in language [...], but language is also at the centre of reason's misunderstanding with itself, in part by reason of the frequent coincidence of major and minor terms, of its vacuity and abundance of ideal phrases, in part because of the infinite number of verbal figures in respect to syllogistic ones [...]." [2]

Kant therefore lived and was formed in an environment in which reflections on language were assigned a decisive function in the construction of thought. The banality of the six or seven pages that the great philosopher devotes to the character of some European languages in his anthropology lessons confirms that Kant never wanted to engage himself in a serious analysis of language and languages.

Kant's silence on language is difficult to interpret. The fact that he never in any way justified it, though living in a climate saturated with problems in the philosophy of language, suggests that this silence is not fortuitous. It may perhaps be thought that, to those who are interested in the apriori, to those who intend to draw up a "systematically ordered inventory of every thing that we possess by virtue of pure reason", language appears as a somewhat intrusive reality. Linguistic forms have no interest for thinkers like Kant because they seem too irredeemably accidental in their being and becoming, too much the daughters of time and transience, too human in their vacillations and incoherencies, too much bound to the individual, too limited to be necessary and universal. The silence of the philosopher of apriori synthesis is perhaps the highest tribute ever paid to the irreducibly historical character of language. It is also possible that Kant, reading Hume and Hamann, suspected the existence of an explosive charge hidden in unrestricted reflections on language: a charge capable of destroying the foundations of every theory of the apriori and universal concepts, considered as such.

Whatever the ways of interpreting Kant's silence, it is certain that it had a decisive effect on the history of later European thought. Naturally, not all nineteenth-century philosophers accepted the solutions Kant proposed, but they largely accepted the problems. The range of interest of European philosophy became bounded by the horizons of the three *Critiques*. Kant's silence caused language to be neglected in philosophical discussion for over a century. The efforts of Bacon and Locke, of Leibniz and Vico, of Berkeley, Hume, Hamann and Herder to build a new theory of language and meaning in the place of Aristotelian, Scholastic and Cartesian theories were not followed up and were forgotten, as we have seen, by the historians of philosophy themselves. (This is a paradoxical confirmation of Croce's thesis on the coincidence of philosophy and history of philosophy.)

The disinterest of philosophers in language and meaning was confirmed by what happened in the field of scientific linguistics. This gradually lost the sense of its historical and ideal origins, and with it all systematic interest in the syntactic and semantic functions of linguistic forms.

The linguistic generation of the mid-nineteenth century was still aware of the eighteenth century origins of linguistic research and of the semantic and philosophical motives behind them. In 1866 BRÉAL (vol. I, pp. VIII–XI) could still write about Bopp's *Vergleichende Grammatik*:

"After Leibniz, who had so many profound and correct views on this subject, Herder taught the Germans to think of languages as something more than simple tools for the exchange of ideas: he showed that they also include, for those who know how to examine them, the oldest and most genuine testimonies of a people's way of thinking and feeling. The Lyceum at

Aschaffenburg had hired some of the teachers of the University of Mayence and there Bopp had one of Herder's admirers, Karl Windischmann, as a teacher [...]. Eastern religions and languages greatly interested Windischmann: like the two Schlegels, like Creuzer and Görres, with whom he shared many ideas, he expected revealing data on the origins of the human race from more complete knowledge of Persia and India [...]. Impelled by these motives, Bopp decided to approach the Orientalists of Paris. A work which has remained famous, a work which loses itself in a thick fog of hypotheses after the first few chapters, but whose beginning must have held the greatest interest to a philologist, certainly influenced this decision. This was Frederick Schlegel's book *On the Language and Wisdom of the Hindus*. In spite of its numerous errors, it may be said that this work fittingly opened the era of Sanskrit studies in Europe." [3]

These passages from Bréal are notable, not only because they show what knowledge of the origins of linguistic enquiries some philologists still possessed even in the mid-nineteenth century; they also well illustrate the hesitation and doubt with which the generation of philologists following Schlegel and Bopp looked at a part of the work done between the end of the eighteenth and the beginning of the nineteenth centuries. A part of these studies began to seem "a thick fog of hypotheses". In fact in Leibniz and in Vico an interest in the historicity of meanings and a consequent interest in the study of language mingled with the hope that the original *forma mentis* of humanity might be discovered by studies of language and meaning. In origin, linguistic enquiries were thus linked to the "Ur"-myth of the ancient wisdom of the human race (ARENS, 1955, pp. 78, 82).

In the work of Hamann and Herder this myth was linked to another, that of the wisdom of the Orient. The Orient is the treasure-house of primitive human wisdom. The two myths become one in Schlegel's work. The study of language does not become the study of external linguistic forms, but that of inner linguistic form and is concentrated on archaic dead languages in order to reconstruct the mother of languages, "Indo-Germanic", or "Indo-European". Knowledge of this archaic tongue gives the linguist access to the treasures of ancient and oriental wisdom. In other words, the analysis of meaning got entangled in mythological speculation about this wisdom.

Bopp was attracted to linguistic studies by the fascination of just this sort of speculation (BRÉAL, 1866, p. IX): but it is likely that he was then aware of the uncertain nature of the results which could be obtained in this direction. This assumption gains credence from the fact that Bopp

19

was interested largely in the formal aspect of linguistic forms in the *Vergleichende Grammatik*, leaving syntactic and semantic analysis in the background. (Bréal specifically noted the absence of syntax in Bopp's work: BRÉAL, p. LXIff.) Doubts over the validity of the enquiries of Fr. Schlegel and Humboldt were consolidated by Pott. MEILLET (1937, p. 462) has observed that a new path in linguistic enquiries opens with Pott.

> "Pott, eleven years younger than Bopp, profited by the work of his fore-runners but he chose his own field, etymology, at the very beginning and studied it in an independent fashion [...]. Without rules of correspondence between related languages, etymology is only a game of the mind in which no proofs can be produced; Pott realised this and wrote the following decisive sentences as early as 1833: 'The alphabetic letters are surer guides in the maze of etymology than is meaning, which is liable to make daring leaps'; and again 'Grimm's exposition of phonetical transformation in the Germanic languages is of more value in itself than several philosophies of language'." [4]

These are indeed "decisive sentences": they are the first tangible expressions of a double attitude which has remained characteristic of historical linguistics: aversion to general principles and to questions about lexical or syntactic meaning. Early mistakes in general theory and semantics alienated the majority of linguists from these fields. Phonetics and morphology were preferred.

It is not easy to demonstrate the presence of this attitude in traditional comparative philology because explicit pronouncements on the subject are rare. (For a philologist it is obvious that the study of language is the study of phonological or morphological patterns and aspects. Moreover, an explicit pronouncement on the subject would in fact be a statement of general principles!) It may of course be recalled that even Meillet, one of the few historical linguists to be interested in general linguistics, once claimed, appealing to experience, that one new well-analysed fact contributes more to the progress of science than ten volumes of theory, no matter how good the theory.

And one of the few historical linguists to work on syntax *ex professo*, Jakob Wackernagel, on at least one occasion also made clear his lack of interest in the semantic value of words from an etymological standpoint (WACKERNAGEL, 1953, p. 1306; but see also Pagliaro's decided reaction to this antisemantic attitude: PAGLIARO, 1961, p. 43). In traditional historical and comparative linguistics, however, the fear of semantics is often seen in the atrophy of syntactic and semantic studies rather than in explicit theoretical positions. Thousands of articles, studies and books were devoted to the diachronic and comparative study of phonematic and grammatical systems of various languages and to tracing words back to their Indo-European roots. But studies of the syntactic and semantic use and functions of forms are relatively rare.

It is all very well to say that also here there is a perfect continuity between traditional comparative philology and structural linguistics. This continuity is often based upon the fact that comparative and historical linguistics of the later nineteenth century perceived the need to think of linguistic facts as integrated in a "system" or "organism" (SOMMERFELT, 1952, p. 77ff; LEPSCHY, 1961, p. 178ff). But the "a-semanticism" of linguistic analysis – be it "traditional" or "modern" – is, in reality, an even more important element of continuity. Formed in the comparative and historical school, traditional linguistics turns its enquiries to diachronic and comparative analyses of phonemic and morphemic structures. Structural linguistics considers the same things from a synchronic point of view. Both tend to neglect the systematic study of semantic and syntactic functions; both agree that "letters are surer guides than meaning". The only noticeable difference is that this a-semantic and anti-semantic attitude is more often explicitly formulated and discussed by modern structural and distributional linguists.

The goal of describing linguistic forms "without any mention of mind or meaning" is for example explicitly proposed by BLOCH (1948, p. 5), HARRIS (1951, pp. 5, 189, 365 etc.), MANDELBROT (1957, pp. 12, 73). This proposal has often been considered "exaggerated" (HALL JR., 1950, p. 288) and has been criticized (MARTINET, 1950, pp. 84–87; FREI, 1954, pp. 136–45; HOCKETT, 1958, pp. 137–39; BELARDI, 1959, p. 127ff). Harris himself is, moreover, aware of the theoretical difficulties facing anyone seeking completely to eliminate recourse to meaning in formal analysis (see Harris' quotations in MOUNIN, 1963, pp. 32–35). It is, however, to be noted that critics of the anti-semantic approach admit recourse to meaning above all as a heuristic criterion for the delimitation and distinction of forms. But the majority of them are far from blaming the distributionalists for not concerning themselves with semantics. In other words, both those who deny the utility or need of looking at meaning in analyzing linguistic forms and those who support it, turn in preference – the latter no less than the former – to the formalistic (phonological and morphological) study of languages, neglecting syntactic and semantic studies.

Traditional historical and comparative linguistics and structural and distributional linguistics thus concur in giving only a minimal part of their

21

energies to a study of the syntactic and semantic aspects of language. But, just as, on the theoretical level, it has been accepted that it is impossible to exclude recourse to meaning as a heuristic criterion for the delimitation and distinction of forms, so interest in syntax and semantics has not been completely extinguished on the level of historical research. And, just as on the theoretical level recourse to meaning is a matter of approximation (that is undoubtedly not the logical but the practical strong point of formalist linguistics) with only minimum consideration of what the meaning of a form may be, so in historical research the rare and atrophic expositions of syntax and semantics are a-critical and approximative. There are of course exceptions. But the majority of the big historical grammars from the late nineteenth century onwards and this century's textbooks of descriptive structural grammar either leave the syntax and semantics of the language studied completely aside or refer to these subjects uncritically. Absurd or irrelevant definitions of "part of speech" or of verbal transitiveness come to mind (see GLINZ, 1947, *passim*, and DE MAURO, 1959).

This neglect has had serious consequences. The ideas of Francis Bacon, Locke, Leibniz, Vico, Hamann, Herder and W. von Humboldt on the historical variable character of complexes of meaning and of syntactic functions succeeded in arousing a new interest in linguistic studies, but they never attained integration in an organic whole of positive and adequate analyses. From Pott onwards, the formalistic tendencies of scientific linguistics restricted every effort in that direction. It was, however, still necessary to discuss syntax and meaning at certain levels, in the schools, in the exegesis of texts, in textbooks and dictionaries. To this end the Aristotelian and Cartesian grammatical tradition, from the time of the Stoics and Priscianus to the grammarians of Port-Royal, had built up an impressive body of doctrine and an abundant terminology. So, at a scholastic and practical level, ancient syntactic and semantic theories continued to exist, and "scientific" syntaxes and theories of meaning accepted this bundle of Aristotelian ideas, by sheer inertia, from the schools. The ancient theory of language as a list of labels, as a mirror of a world of things and concepts existing prior to language, and the theory of the proposition as a picture of a fact, thus re-emerged and was able to dominate syntax and semantics (GLINZ, 1947, p. 75; LEROY, 1963, pp. 13–14).

As has been mentioned, because of the "Kantian" disinterest of philosophers and historians of philosophy in language and in previous philosophy of language it was forgotten that the theory of vocabulary as a repertory of labels and of the proposition as a picture had been criticized and shown to be false by some of the great European thinkers of the seventeenth and eighteenth centuries. So a philosopher's neglect of the problems of language and the a-critical Aristotelianism and rationalism of the linguists combined in such a way that Aristotelian ideas on language were still predominant in European linguistic research at the end of the nineteenth century. Such basic attainments of modern culture as the disappearance of verbalism, the advent of the experimental method, the discovery of semantic and syntactical internal differences of languages, the observations and theories of Bacon, Locke, Leibniz, Vico, might as well never have been. The very naïve conception which Martinet today criticizes dominated, strengthened by the common sense and culture of the time and by its uncritical acceptance on the part of linguistic specialists.

The contribution of those who, at the beginning of this century, called the attention of philosophy and linguistics back to the general problems of language and meaning should be seen against this background of the lifeless and mechanical repetition of the ideas of a venerable antiquity. We can today share or reject the ideas of Croce, Saussure or Wittgenstein. In any case, it cannot be denied that the greatest merit of these three men is that they posed arguments and problems which had not been discussed since the eighteenth century. Of the three, Wittgenstein began by taking the most difficult way of undermining the traditional conceptions of the linguistic facts: Croce and Saussure, as we shall observe later, assumed an aggressive attitude towards tradition from the beginning (even if in actual fact they did not succeed in discarding it completely); the early Wittgenstein worked from the total acceptance of traditional ideas. But, accepting them, he gave them a formal rigour in which they had never been cast, not even by Aristotle. In this way he laid bare their most secret links and exposed all the consequences logically deriving from them to the limits of absurdity, indeed – and here lies his merit – beyond absurdity.

NOTES

[1] Descartes, *Opera*, ed. A.T., vol. VIII (Paris 1905), p. 8 (=*Principia Philosophiae*, I, X): "Non hic explico alia multa nomina, quibus jam usus sum, vel utor in sequentibus, quia per se satis nota mihi videntur. Et saepe adverti philosophos in hoc errare, quod ea, quae simplicissima erant ac per se nota, Logicis definitionibus explicare conarentur; ita enim ipsa obscuriora reddebant. Atque ubi dixi hanc propositionem, *ego cogito, ergo*

sum, esse omnium primam ac certissimam, quae cuilibet ordine philosophari occurrat, non ideo negavi quin ante ipsam scire oporteat, quid sit *cogitatio*, quid *existentia*, quid *certitudo* [...]; sed quia hae sunt simplicissimae notiones [...], idcirco non censui esse numerandas."

2 "So braucht es keiner Deduktion, die genealogische Priorität der Sprache vor der sieben heiligen Funktionen logischer Sätze und Schlüsse und ihre Heraldik zu beweisen. Nicht nur das ganze Vermögen zu denken beruht auf der Sprache [...]: sondern Sprache ist auch der Mittelpunkt des Mißverstandes der Vernunft mit ihr selbst, theils wegen der häufigen Coincidenz des größten und kleinsten Begriffs, seiner Leere und Fülle in idealischen Sätzen, theils wegen des unendlichen Bereichs der Rede – vor den Schluß-figuren [...]."

3 "Après Leibniz, qui eut sur ce sujet tant de vues profondes et justes, Herder avait appris à l'Allemagne à considérer les langues autrement que comme de simples instruments destinés à l'échange des idées: il avait montré qu'elles renferment aussi, pour qui sait les interroger, les témoignages les plus anciens et les plus authentiques sur la façon de penser et de sentir des peuples. Au lycée de Aschaffenbourg, qui avait en partie recueilli les professeurs de l'Université de Mayence, M. Bopp eut pour maître un admirateur de Herder, Charles Windischmann [...]. Les religions et les langues de l'Orient étaient un objet de vive curiosité: comme les deux Schlegel, comme Creuzer, et Goerres, avec lesquels il était en communauté d'idée, il attendait d'une connaissance plus complète de la Perse et de l'Inde des révélations sur le commencements du genre humain. Un ouvrage resté célèbre, qui se perd, après les premiers chapitres, dans un épais brouillard d'hypotheses, mais dont le commencement devait offrir le plus vif interêt à l'esprit d'un linguiste, ne fût sans doute pas étranger à cette décision. Nous voulons parler du livre de Frédéric Schlegel *Sur la langue et la sagesse des Indous*. Malgré des nombreuses erreurs, on peut dire que ce travail ouvrait dignement l'ère des études sanscrites en Europe."

4 "Pott, de onze ans plus jeune que Bopp, a profité des travaux de ses devanciers, mais il s'est choisi dès l'abord son domaine, l'étymologie, et il y a travaillé d'une manière indépendante [...]. Sans règles de correspondances entre les langues rapprochées, l'étymologie n'est qu'un jeu d'esprit et ne comporte pas de démonstrations; Pott l'a vu, et dès 1833, il écrit ces phrases décisives: 'La lettre est un guide plus sûr dans le labyrinthe de l'étymologie que la signification, souvent sujette aux sautes les plus hardis' et 'l'exposition qu'a faite Grimm des transformations phonétiques dans les langues germaniques a plus de valeur à elle seule que plusieurs philosophies du language'."

CHAPTER IV

LANGUAGE AS NOMENCLATURE AND
WITTGENSTEIN'S LINGUISTIC SOLIPSISM

The *Tractatus* opens with a solemn sequence of ontological assertions. "The world is all that is the case" (1), it "is the totality of facts" (1.2), that is, it "divides into facts" (1.2). A fact "is the existence of states of affairs" (2) and "a state of affairs (a state of things) is a combination of objects (things)" (2.01). Since they are part of the world, pictures cannot be considered other than "facts" (2.141). But they are facts of a particular kind; they are facts which have something in common with other facts: "If a fact is to be a picture, it must have something in common with what it depicts" (2.16). This "something" is what Wittgenstein calls "form", "pictorial form" (2.171). Pictorial form is the possibility that the elements of the picture are related to one another (i.e. they have a structure) in the same way (i.e. with the same structure) as the things (objects) in a fact (2.15, 2.151).

One of the things Wittgenstein wishes to make clear is that it is not necessary for a picture to represent the fact of which it is a picture iconically in order to be such. The necessary and sufficient condition is that the articulations of the picture follow the articulations of the represented fact. This conclusion is important if we are to understand the propositions of phonic language as a particular case of pictures (this was, as has been said, Wittgenstein's aim). In fact, "at first sight a proposition – one set out on the printed page, for example – does not seem to be a picture of the reality with which it is concerned. But no more does musical notation at first sight seem to be a picture of music, nor our phonetic notation (the alphabet) to be a picture of our speech" (4.011). What makes a proposition a picture of the fact with which it is concerned is its articulation (3.251), its having a structure identical with the structure of the fact. It is this identity of structures (that is of the relations between the elements composing them) which allows us to say that "a proposition is a picture of reality" (4.01). It is "a projection of a possible situation" (3.11), whose elements, or "simple signs", are names (3.202). Each name means an object: the object is the meaning of each name (3.203). To the

25

configuration of names in the propositional sign corresponds the con-figuration of objects in a situation (3.21). As a consequence of this corre-spondence, an object cannot be imagined as divorced from combinations with other objects in states of affairs (2.021), so that "only in the nexus of a proposition does a name have any meaning" (3.3), that is, only in a proposition does a name correspond to a determined object. From this it follows that a name cannot be defined alone (3.26), outside a proposition.

It may seem strange that Wittgenstein should go to the length of stating such banalities. And there is no doubt that they are banalities: if we are to understand all the greatness of Wittgenstein we must also understand that the above phrases are extremely trite. They do no more than restate the "conception superficielle du grand public" to which SAUSSURE (1922, p. 34) referred, the same "very naïve, but widespread conception" of which MARTINET (1960, pp. 14–15) writes, i.e. the old Aristotelian and rationalist conception of the world and of the linguistic facts. But, as may be seen, Wittgenstein expounds an extremely rigorous version of this conception, one that is completely explicit in all its logical impli-cations. It is this very rigour, this clarity, which allows Wittgenstein to build up the limpid and irrefutable paradox expressed in proposition 3.263 of the *Tractatus*.

As Wittgenstein already said, "a name [...] is a primitive sign". Now, "the meanings of primitive signs can be explained by means of elucidations (*Erläuterungen*)". But what are these elucidations? "Elucidations are propositions that contain the primitive signs." But these propositions, like all propositions, "can only be understood if the meaning of those signs are already known".

It clearly is a closed circle. Understanding propositions presupposes the understanding of the names composing them. But understanding the names presupposes the understanding of the propositions containing them. A proposition is understood (as is a name) only if it is already understood. It follows that man never goes beyond the limits of his own language, he does not communicate, he lives in the seclusion of his language and of his world.

"*The limits of my language* mean the limits of my world" (5.6).

"The world is *my* world: this is manifest in the fact that the limits of *language* (of that language which alone I understand) mean the limits of *my* world" (5.62)

Wittgenstein was a man of rigorous consistency, not unrelated to his

26

religious experiences of a mystical nature, which almost led him, at one time, to decide to become a monk, and give away all his possessions (BARONE, 1953, p. 162; MALCOLM, 1958, pp. 10–11). With similar consistency he wrote, in the preface to the *Tractatus*: "Perhaps this book will be understood only by someone who has himself had the thoughts that are expressed in it". It was not a *boutade*. The extreme stand he reaches in the *Tractatus* is expressed in these words. Only a mystic communion of souls (that is, a communion non demonstrable empirically or rationally) guarantees that the meaning of a phrase be understood by someone other than the person uttering it. Failing this, communication is impossible.

If thinking aimed only at arriving at true or false propositions, we could only say that the conclusions of the early Wittgenstein are false. They do not in fact succeed in explaining how it is that "with propositions, however, we make ourselves understood" (4.026) and how "it belongs to the essence of a proposition that it should be able to communicate a *new* sense to us" (4.027). Wittgenstein's conclusions contrast with these two propositions and, what is worse, are in contradiction with the facts expressed by them. The philosopher who denied the existence of movement was very simply answered: his listener got up and, without saying a word, walked away. We can answer anyone who denies the possibility of communicating in the same way: by speaking to each other, communicating our thoughts to others and understanding theirs.

We know, however, that the philosopher who denied the possibility of movement was in actual fact making a different point. The object of his denial was not movement but one particular conception of it. His negation of movement served history as a demonstration that, *if* movement is conceived in a certain way and with certain premises, *then* it must logically be deduced that movement is not possible. His negation was thus useful in making science move towards a new and better conception of movement and space. Similarly, Wittgenstein's absurd solipsistic conclusion was useful in stimulating the quest for a new way of conceiving language and its relations with the world and with men. This is the real meaning and value of the thought of the early Wittgenstein. *If* we believe that language is a repertory of labels, that propositions are projections of states of things, *then* we must conclude that language and propositions cannot communicate meanings to people.

The historical importance of the *Tractatus* is a revision of the Aristotelian and rationalistic conception of language and propositions. This revision, its necessity, and the research it involved, are the most precious legacy of the early Wittgenstein's linguistic theories. Not a treasure, but the thrill of finding it. Not a patrimony of realized truths, but one of the truths to be realized. It is a legacy which in its "form" (in Wittgenstein's sense of the word) resembles, indeed is identical with, the legacy of the early Croce and of Saussure.

CHAPTER V

LINGUISTIC SOLIPSISM IN CROCE AND SAUSSURE

As it has been maintained of the early Wittgenstein, it has also been said of the early Croce that his statements did not concern the whole of language and all propositions but only part of them, that is only the "pre-grammatical *parole*" (DEVOTO, 1953) or only language in its aesthetic function (COSERIU, 1962, p. 31ff). However, as in the case of Wittgenstein, it is easy to see that also Croce's statements on language were meant to refer to the whole of language and to every proposition (DE MAURO, 1964, p. 183ff). Unlike Wittgenstein, Croce from the beginning adopted a polemic attitude towards traditional ideas about language, which seemed to him bound to an *entificatio*, to a substantialization of abstractions. Each linguistic expression is an individual entity and cannot be realistically described in terms of general categories (CROCE, 1899–1900; 1951, pp. 2–9, 13–15). He (1902, p. 76) writes:

"Single expressive facts are so many individuals, the one not to be equalled to another except in their quality of being expressions [...]. The impressions, i.e. the contents, vary; every content is different from every other because nothing in life is repeated; and to the variations in contents corresponds the irreducible variety of expressive forms, that is of the aesthetic synthesis of impressions." [1]

Later he states (1910, p. 159):

"Language is only a series of expressions, each one of which appears in the form in which it appears, only once." [2]

But if this is so, if each linguistic expression, each proposition appears in the way it does only once, and can be neither repeated nor compared with others, how can we explain the process of communication? The Neapolitan philosopher had no sympathy for the "mystics of the ineffable" (CROCE, 1908, pp. 10–11). All the same did not his positions carried to their extremes, cast before them the shadows of incommunicability? A friend and follower of Croce, Karl Vossler, did in fact once raise this doubt (VOSSLER, 1908, pp. 113–14). Thirty years later, before Croce worked out his "second" theory of language and linguistics, a similar doubt was expressed to Croce by Silvio Ceccato, who asked how it was possible to explain that a certain expression communicated a certain content on the bases of the linguistic ideas set out in the *Aesthetics* (ROSSI-LANDI, 1961, p. 240). In fact, in Croce's universe as in Wittgenstein's, statements follow one another without the possibility of communication being justified or admitted: speech appears as a lyrical expression by means of signs which cannot be repeated. For Croce as for Wittgenstein, the only guarantee of effective communication between humans is to be found beyond the limits of reason and experience, in the realms of the "Absolute Spirit": according to CROCE (1941, vol. I, p. 235) "the problem of mutual understanding between speakers has lost the veil of mystery which surrounded it because it has been transferred to the concept of the Spirit, universal-individual, which is intrinsically communication and society of beings among themselves".[3] We must therefore repeat that in Croce's first linguistic theories only the mystic communion of souls guarantees that the meaning of a proposition be understood by a person other than the speaker. Otherwise, for the early Croce communication is wrapped in a "mysterious veil".

There will of course be those linguists who, intent on the discovery of some etymology, or on explaining why Italian geminated consonants are geminated and not intense (or vice versa), will find new reasons for not concerning themselves with questions of principle and for sticking to "concrete facts". But what is a "concrete fact" in linguistics? After Saussure, this is the pressing question. As Leroy has aptly noted, after Saussure linguistics can no longer limit itself to collecting "concrete" facts (LEROY, 1963, p. 60; see also LEPSCHY, 1961, p. 197).

After Godel's fundamental work (GODEL, 1957) on the manuscript sources of the *Cours de linguistique générale*, the logical and psychological starting point of Saussure's thought is clear. In 1894, on the subject of Lettish intonation Saussure (quoted in GODEL, 1957, p. 31) wrote to Meillet:

"But I am disgusted with all this, and with the difficulty one generally finds in writing even ten lines on the facts of language with any common sense at all. For a long time I have been principally concerned with the logical classification of these facts, with the classification of the points of view from which we treat them. But I see with increasing clarity the immense amount of work necessary to show a linguist *what he is doing* [...] Unceasingly, this inadequacy

30

of current terminology, the necessity of reforming it, and this of showing what language is in general, are spoiling my historical pleasure although I have no dearer wish than that of not having to work on general linguistics. In spite of myself all this will end up with a book, in which, without enthusiasm, I shall explain why there is not one term used in linguistics to which I grant any meaning whatsoever [...]." [4]

Saussure realized that he was the only one aware of the problem. In the *Cours* (SAUSSURE, 1922, p. 153) we read:

"Linguistics works unceasingly with concepts made by the grammarians and we do not know if they really correspond to the constituent factors of the system of language." [5]

This need for clarity, for precision (which he explicitly revealed to Riedlinger: GODEL, 1957, p. 25) drove Saussure to ask the fundamental question of all linguistic thought from Aristotle to the eighteenth century. What is it that makes a word a word, a phrase a phrase, a linguistic form a linguistic form? As GODEL (1957, p. 136ff) observed, this problem, i.e., the problem of the identity, is at the core of Saussure's thought. Saussure was a historical linguist who was also the creator of static linguistics: in his eyes the problem has two dimensions, one diachronic and one synchronic.

In diachronic linguistics we say for example that the Latin *cantare* becomes the French *chanter*, or that the Common German **fōti* becomes English *feet*. Such a statement presupposes that there is a continuity between *cantare* and *chanter*, between **foti* and *feet* (quoted in GODEL, 1957, p. 68). Something must remain the same if we are to be able to say that something has changed. Actually, Saussure observes (GODEL, 1957, p. 48) that in historical linguistics

"We speak of phenomena which occur between such and such terms, as if these terms were no more to be defined than any visible object, as if it were not the terms themselves which should first be defined. It is a fiction. The most controversial point of linguistics consists precisely in understanding how a term is brought into existence, since none is given to us as an entirely clear entity, apart from the illusion created by habit." [6]

But the same problem arises in synchrony: "What does the identity of a word (for example, *Messieurs*) pronounced twice rest on?" [7]

The problem of the identity of linguistic forms was faced before Saussure (and sometimes after him too) and mainly two types of solutions have been suggested, one according to form and one in terms of content.

Formalists say: the identity of a linguistic form is guaranteed by the identity of the phonetic material of which it is constructed. (It could easily be shown that the definitions of linguistic unity in general and of phonemes in particular put forward by Jones, Pike and Harris can be ultimately reduced to this thesis. But this is not the place for it.) This claim is extremely weak. If identity is to be based on phonetic criteria, it should be noted that two linguistic forms (phrases, words, phonemes), however similar, are never acoustically identical. What we call "the same phrase", "the same phoneme" is never exactly identical, from an acoustic point of view, on two different occasions (ZIFF-DE MAURO, 1963, pp. 30–32). The reasons for identification cannot be found in pure acoustics neither from a synchronic point of view nor (and even less) from a diachronic one. Saussure understood this very well (quotations in GODEL, 1957, p. 45) and firmly refused any formalistic solution in all his writings.

Supporters of the content point of view claim precisely this: a word is never identical to itself from the acoustic point of view, all the same it is and remains the same because it always has the same meaning (quotations in GODEL, 1957, p. 45). This claim, however, is extremely weak too. It might be acceptable if we could comprehend the meaning independently of the word expressing it. But then language would be a nomenclature. Saussure is clearly aware that this is not so. The nexus of acoustic images and meaning "is liable to suffer displacements over time which the logician cannot account for" (quoted in GODEL, 1957, p. 45). In principle, moreover, meaning (*signifié*) cannot be grasped except in relation to signifying form (*signifiant*: SAUSSURE, 1922, pp. 98ff, 155ff; GODEL, 1957, pp. 137, 139–40).

Having rejected the formalistic solution and the solution in terms of content to the problem of the identity of linguistic forms, Saussure proposes a third and new solution. What makes the various occurrences of a word variants of the same linguistic unity is that they always have the same linguistic "value" (quoted in GODEL, 1957, p. 139). As in chess, so in language for a given element one can ask (quoted in GODEL, 1957, p. 139):

"Does it have an identity? Absolutely, insofar as it has a value. One notes that not only every other knight, but even figures which have no resemblance to a knight, provided they are different from all the others, are considered identical in a chess game, provided they have the same value." [8]

Only difference in value allows us to distinguish two entities as homophones (*pas* as a substantive and *pas* as a negation, for example) or as variants of the same word (GODEL, 1957, p. 139). This, however, does not yet adequately take care of the question of identity. What is it in fact that guarantees identity of value?

Saussure seeks an answer to this problem in the notion of "system". The identity of a linguistic form depends on its value, and its value depends on the linguistic system of which this form is a part. The value of an element in inflexion or of a word is determined and guaranteed by its relations to the other elements or words in the system of which it is a part. Saussure (in GODEL, 1957, p. 225) writes:

> "All magnitudes depend upon each other; (all signs are solidary): do we want to decide what *jugement* is in French? We can only define it by what is around it, be it to decide what it is in itself, be it to decide what it is not."

Hence the need to consider the sign in the system as a whole.[9] GODEL (1957, p. 139ff) analyses the formulations Saussure gives to this solution very carefully. There is no doubt that one finds hesitations and obscurities in them, and with very good reason: a thinker as rigorous as Saussure could not be satisfied with such a solution.

If the identity, and hence the linguistic usefulness, of a form depends on its value, and if this in its turn is determined by the system, various antinomical and paradoxical consequences follow. An antinomical result was certainly half foreseen by Saussure himself. Linguistic forms are defined according to the relationship which binds them, as has been said. But how can the relationships be defined without having defined the *relata*? GODEL (1957, p. 221) comments: "Linguistics thus finds itself in a vicious circle"[10].

But there are two other paradoxical consequences. It has been noted (LUCIDI, 1966, p. 169ff.) that Saussure's definition of linguistic unity prevents our explaining how two successive linguistic stages can be compared. Let us take an everyday example. If we accept the Saussurian definition in all its rigour, the word *gatta* "cat" in Old Italian would not be comparable with the word *gatta* "she-cat" in Modern Italian, since the latter coexists with the word *gatto* "tom-cat", a form unknown in Old Italian. We could establish a continuity between the two words only if we admitted that not only the relationship with other words, but something independent of their relationships with other words is essential and constitutive to them. If we believe with Saussure that the essence of a word is determined by its relations with other idiosynchronic words, since

33

the relationships of the Old Italian *gatta* are different from those of the Modern Italian *gatta*, then the first and second *gatta* would be two *completely* different words, as different as *gatta* and *elefante* or *dinosauro*. It would therefore be neither sensible nor legitimate to talk about the transformation, or the phonological or semantic change, of the word *gatta* – it would make just as much sense to talk about the transformation in form and meaning of the word *gatta* into the word *elefante* or *dinosauro*. As a general rule, Saussure's definition of linguistic unity makes it impossible to explain on what the comparison or the connecting links between two successive stages of the same element or of an entire linguistic system are based. Mario Lucidi considered that it was in fact because Saussure saw this difficulty that he never published his work in definitive form.

As Godel has observed, the problem of diachronic identity is no more than a complicated variant of the problem of synchronic identity (GODEL, 1957, p. 138). Godel's comment suggests that the absurd consequences to be drawn from Saussure's premises from the diachronic point of view also result from the synchronic one. In other words, Saussure's premises not only do not allow us to justify or explain the relation of diachronic continuity of two successive stages of the same language, but they do not even explain how two or more people can say that they speak the same language nor how they can understand each other. For Saussure, the presence or absence of a single word changes the whole play of relationships in a lexical system. GODEL (1957, p. 229) writes:

"In the second course, as in the interview with A. Riedlinger, language is defined as a *closely-knit* system (système *serré*), and the epithet is thus explained: '*Closely-knit* implies precision of values (the least nuance changes words); variety in the kind of values; an immense variety of terms, of the unities involved in the system; strict and reciprocal dependence of the unities among themselves: everything in a language is syntactical, everything is a system." [11]

If only relationships count, the vocabulary of Huxley's character who did not know the word *carminative* is different from that of others who did know the word. Even the smallest differences in the vocabularies of two people (and we know that such differences are in fact considerable: MILLER, 1951, pp. 165–170) would force us to conclude, if we wanted to be loyal to Saussure's premises, that the two spoke different languages and that even the words that they apparently had in common were in reality only homophonic, having different values because they occurred in two

34

different sets of relationships. It is clear why Saussure at least once felt the need of defining the relation between thought and sound in language as "a somewhat mysterious thing" ("un fait en quelque sort mystérieux": SAUSSURE, 1922, p. 156). Even the notion of a system does not really allow us to explain this relation – and, hence, the process of communication – satisfactorily. Indeed, if carried to its ultimate consequences Saussure's theory of 'system' leads to the conclusion that two people can only communicate if their vocabularies are totally identical.

Linguistic solipsism, explicitly asserted by the early Wittgenstein is therefore implicit not only in Croce's philosophy of language, that is in an idealistic and spiritualistic philosophy, but also in Saussure. A shadow of mystery hovers over the process of communication, be it seen with the eyes of Croce, Saussure or Wittgenstein.

NOTES

[1] "I singoli fatti espressivi sono altrettanti individui, l'uno non ragguagliabile coll'altro se non nella comune qualità di espressione [...]. Variano le impressioni ossia i contenuti; ogni contenuto è diverso da ogni altro, perchè niente si ripete nella vita; e al variare dei contenuti corrisponde la varietà irriducibile delle forme espressive, sintesi estetica delle impressioni".

[2] "[E che cosa è] la lingua se non una serie di espressioni, di cui ciascuna appare in quel modo che appare una volta sola [?]".

[3] "Il problema del reciproco intendersi dei parlanti ha perduto il velo misterioso che l'avvolgeva, perchè è stato riportato al concetto dello Spirito, universale e individuale, che è intrinsecamente comunicazione e società degli esseri tra loro."

[4] "Mais je suis bien dégoûté de tout cela, et de la difficulté qu'il y a en général à écrire seulement dix lignes ayant le sens commun en matière de faits de langage. Préoccupé surtout depuis longtemps de la classification logique de ces faits, de la classification des points de vue sous lesquels nous les traitons, je vois de plus en plus à la fois l'immensité du travail qu'il faudrait pour montrer au linguiste *ce qu'il fait*. ... Sans cesse, cette ineptie de la terminologie courante, la nécessité de la réformer, et de montrer pour cela quelle espèce d'objet est la langue en général, vient gâter mon plaisir historique, quoique je n'aie pas de plus cher voeu que de ne pas avoir à m'occuper de la langue en général. Cela finira malgré moi par un livre où, sans enthousiasme, j'expliquerai pourquoi il n'y a pas un seul terme employé en linguistique auquel j'accorde un sens quelconque [...]."

[5] "La linguistique travaille sans cesse sur des concepts forgés par les grammairiens, et dont on ne sait s'ils correspondent réellement à des facteurs constitutifs du système de la langue."

[6] "Nous parlons des phénomènes qui se passent entre tels et tels termes, comme si ces termes n'avaient pas plus à être définis que n'importe quel objet visible, n'étaient pas eux-mêmes ce qu'il faudrait d'abord définir. C'est une fiction. C'est justement le point le plus délicat de la linguistique que de se rendre compte de ce qui fait l'existence d'un terme quelconque, car aucun ne nous est donné comme un genre d'entité tout clair, si ce n'est par l'illusion que nous procure l'habitude."

[7] "Sur quoi fait-on reposer l'identité … d'un mot (*Messieurs*) prononcé deux fois?"

[8] "A-t-il une identité? Totalement, dans la mesure où il aura une valeur. On constate que non seulement tout autre cavalier, mais que même des figures qui n'auraient aucune ressemblance avec le cavalier, pourvu qu'elles diffèrent de toutes autres, seront déclarées identiques pour le jeu d'échecs, pourvu qu'elles aient même valeur."

[9] "Toutes les grandeurs dépendent les unes des autres; (tous les signes sont solidaires): veut-on déterminer en français ce qu'est 'jugement'? On ne peut le définir que par ce qui l'entoure, soit pour dire ce qu'il est en lui-même, soit pour dire ce qu'il n'est pas. … De là apparaît la nécessité de considérer le signe dans l'ensemble du système."

[10] "La linguistique se trouve ainsi enfermée dans un cercle."

[11] "Dans le cours II, comme aussi dans l'entretien avec A. Riedlinger, la langue est qualifiée de système *serré*, et cette épithète est ainsi commentée: 'Serré implique précision des valeurs (la moindre nuance change les mots); multiplicité des genres de valeurs; multiplicité immense des termes, des unités en jeu dans le système; réciproque et stricte dépendance des unités entre elles: tout est syntactique dans la langue, tout est un système'."

36

CHAPTER VI

SEMANTIC SCEPTICISM IN
CONTEMPORARY LINGUISTICS

The conclusions of the early Wittgenstein, of the early Croce and of Saussure seem to uphold those of linguistic scepticism. They do not agree directly with the scepticism of formalistic linguistics as to the possibilities of studying meaning. That scepticism is, as we have noted above, methodological: it neither says that meaning does not exist nor that linguistic forms have no meaning; it states no more than that, since meaning is an elusive thing, linguistics should ignore it and work only on external descriptions of languages and of linguistic behaviour. We have already noted twice the criticism to which this approach is open. It is impossible to specify and distinguish the linguistic forms to be described without recourse to meaning. (Since the formalistic attitude is sometimes considered typically "American" it is worth remembering that it has not only been criticized by American linguists such as Hall jr. and Hockett but by the very founder of American linguistics, Leonard Bloomfield. BLOOMFIELD, 1933 (pp. 27, 74–75, 138–59) was well aware of the difficulties in studying meaning, but he knew that formal description was not possible without recourse to the criterion of the semantic diversity or identity of forms.) Saussure puts forward good and precise reasons for rejecting formalism and methodological semantic scepticism.

The linguistic scepticism which was strengthened by the early conclusions of Wittgenstein and Croce and from Saussure is not unrelated to existentialistic scepticism. It is foreshadowed in the nineteenth century, but not until the twentieth did it spread from the pages of philosophy to non-philosophical scientific pursuits. According to the existentialists, men do not talk, they chatter. Chatter, *das Gerede*, everyday speech, consists in putting words together, in hearing words, in repeating them, without any real possibility of communication or comprehension. Incommunicability is the normal condition of the man of the street. Silent contemplation of Being and ecstasy of poetry are the only real possibilities of communication (HEIDEGGER, 1935, p. 168ff; 1937, p. 8). As Kierkegaard had said, the only possible society is that of the individual with God, in a relationship in which no other can participate.

In spite of its irrational element, this complete scepticism on the possibilities of communication seems the only reasonable consequence to be drawn from the conclusions of the three greatest twentieth century language theorists.

There are reasons for rejecting these doubts concerning the possibilities of communication: not theoretical or scientific reasons, but practical and human ones. We may consider linguistic communication to be theoretically impossible, but in fact we communicate with our neighbours every day and every hour, and even the supporters of incommunicability successfully communicate the reasons for their ideas and their anguish. These are not valid theoretical reasons, but they are sufficiently consistent, on the practical and human level, to make the theorist seek valid scientific and theoretical ones to explain how men communicate among themselves, and what guarantees that this is possible at all. There is a way to find these reasons and scientifically valid explanation. The Aristotelian conception taken up by Wittgenstein, the linguistic ideas of the early Croce and those of Saussure are very different from each other; but they all lead to sceptical conclusions on the possibilities of communication. We may ask if this common sceptical conclusion is based on a common premise: one which it should be possible to lay bare.

Let us briefly recall the three conceptions. Wittgenstein takes up Aristotle's thesis that the possibilities of communication are or should be guaranteed by the fact that words have a stable meaning. And words have a stable meaning insofar as they are linked by a one-to-one correspondence to the series of ideas and things: this correspondence makes words "the same for everyone". This conception of language as a nomenclature was severely criticized from without by the seventeenth and eighteenth century philosophers, and more recently, by Saussure and Martinet. The early Wittgenstein, however, radically criticized it from within. As we have seen, he shows that if language and proposition are considered mirror-images of objects and events in the world, our propositions can never communicate anything new to other people. Croce rejects the rationalistic interpretations of language and world: to distinguish different words and different classes of objects is, in his opinion, equivalent to submitting realities – which are not in themselves divided – to a process of abstraction. It is not true, for Croce, that propositions are sets of vocables. Propositions are unique and indivisible realities. They have meaning insofar as they are one with their content, with the state of mind they express. One, and only one, state of mind corresponds to each expression, and one expression only to each state of mind. It is clear that according to this conception no misunderstandings are possible since every phrase, every expression, appears only once in history and with its own special meaning. But it is equally clear that this conception does not explain how we communicate as it does not admit an expression and its state of mind to be ever reproduceable, repeatable and, hence, communicable. Saussure believes that the identity of a word's meaning in its several occurrences is guaranteed in that it always has the same value. The permanence of an identical value is in its turn guaranteed by the fact that words are part of a system which, we might say, absorbs the shocks due to the use of words by individuals and gives stability to their value. The systems of two individuals, however, are never perfectly identical through every shade of meaning (it is in any case difficult to prove that two idiolects are perfectly identical): the Saussurian point of view therefore rules out that the same words ever have the same value and the same meaning for two individuals.

The guarantee that linguistic forms have meaning is sought in the linguistic forms themselves in all three conceptions, different though they be. Aristotle and Wittgenstein look for it in linguistic forms in their relations to things, Croce finds it in the relation to their content, and in Saussure it consists in the relation between linguistic forms and the system. It is, in any case, always to linguistic forms that they look. This is the common element of the three theories and, we may say, of all linguistic thought up to the first decades of this century. It is in fact this very element which precludes an adequate explanation of the possibility of communication, and promotes linguistic scepticism; a concrete experiment, that of mechanical translation – or rather, its failure – also confirms this assumption.

Although none of the experiments in mechanical translation has been successful, the research done on the subject has not been useless. It has, first of all, confirmed that the series of meanings and syntactic structures of one language have no precise and ready-to-hand counterparts in others, as was already known at the time of Francis Bacon. But the rediscovery of this forgotten truth has been revealing (see for example CECCATO, 1960, pp. 19–20). Secondly, research on the possibility of mechanical translation has demonstrated something which is both newer and more important. It has shown that a phrase, when isolated from the situation in which it was written or pronounced, can have widely different meanings. This could perhaps have been deduced from isolated historical experience. The elusiveness of *Beati pauperes spiritu, Sapere aude, Le style est l'homme* and so many others are well known: isolated from their original situation they have taken different and even opposite meanings at different times, meanings which were historically illegitimate, but perfectly appropriate linguistically. The experience of research in mechanical translation has shown that such phenomena form part not of the pathology but of the physiology of language. A phrase is not normally plurisemantic for the hearer, but for him the phrase is not isolated: he hears it in a precise setting made up of all he knows about the person who pronounces it, about his past experiences, his plans, about what the author of the phrase knows and thinks about those for whom the phrase is intended, and so forth (see also CECCATO, 1960, p. 19). This enormous bundle of information, not linguistically formalized, helps the rapid selection of the meaning best adapted to the situation in which the phrase was pronounced. Isolated from this framework every phrase may be plurisemantic.

An Italian scholar, who worked on the problems of mechanical translation for many years before leaving this field for richer pastures, recently claimed that the phrase "the spirit is willing but the flesh is weak" – if mechanically translated into Japanese and back again – would become "There is some good whisky, but the roast beef is mediocre". In other words, compared with the naked linguistic form, the machine has no possibility of choosing between the various meanings it possesses. The information we receive from linguistic forms does not depend on them alone, but on them in relation to the speaker and to the non-linguistic situation in which they have their setting. If we phrase it in semiotic terms, we can say that the semantic and syntactic evaluation of a sign should be integrated with its pragmatic evaluation to arrive at its value. More precisely, the semantic-syntactical and the pragmatic evaluation complete each other.

Research on mechanical translation has provided experimental proof that, in themselves, linguistic forms cannot guarantee the transmission of a meaning. They gain this power only in relation to the person using them.

It is interesting to note that Saussure himself took a few, though timid, steps in this direction. GODEL (1957, p. 139) has brought out the fact that the Genevan scholar, in his third and last course in general linguistics, turned back once more to the problem of the identity of linguistic forms, saying (*Cahiers G. Degallier*, p. 196, Biblioth. publ. et univ., Genève, *Cours univ.* 431):

> "It must be admitted that there is here, in judgements on identity or non-identity, a subjective element, though one common to everybody. It is however very difficult to see where there is identity. And our identities are the foundation. The whole mechanism of language turns on identities and differences." [1]

As this brief passage shows, Saussure recognized that linguistic forms draw their value, in the last analysis, not from the system of which they are a part, but from those who use them within a community.

Croce went through a similar development in a later period of his linguistic thought. There is evidence for this as early as 1941 (CROCE, 1941, pp. 241–42):

> What is called language outside its production, contemplation, judgement of expressiveness, the language of linguists [...] must be [...] quite a different thing, something which enters into the moral life of man, among his cravings, his desires, his wishes and actions, his habits, the flights of his imagination, the patterns of his behaviour (and among these also his way of attributing one or another meaning to the sounds he makes and of pronouncing them in one way or another), in everything which in itself is a practical action. [2]

The idea of language as a social praxis, which barely appears in the work cited above, is taken up and developed in a series of later notes which culminate in a study of the nature and purposes of linguistics (CROCE, 1950, pp. 247–53). For reasons of consistency, so as not radically to contradict the ideas he put forward forty years earlier in the *Filosofia dello Spirito*, Croce was not able to develop this idea to the end (DE MAURO, 1954, pp. 386–87; CAVACIUTI, 1959, pp. 92–93; LOMBARDI, 1963, *passim*). This, however, makes it the more interesting that it shows up repeatedly in his later writings. On linguistic studies he asks:

> "What are individual words, the objects of these investigations? I have already suggested, and do so again, that they be called 'signs': phonic, imitative, graphic signs, either combinations of them, or to be examined and classified as you will. And what is the sign?"

Taking up a thesis already set forth elsewhere (CROCE, 1935, pp. 3–8), Croce repeats the distinction between the mere 'symptoms' of a situation and the 'signs'. But the picture which Croce, finally, draws of the origin of such signs is entirely new (1950, pp. 248–49):

"The will and practical action, for those reasons of life which are called those of social communication – and here we must not forget to include in society our own communication with and to ourselves – intervene to fix and elaborate these various symptoms, raising them by their elaboration to be signs [...] as expedients and practical means for recalling things or facts and, so to say, to designate them.[3]

Croce's later work thus recognizes the part played in the process of communication by the will and consensus of individuals as grouped together in associative life. To the later Wittgenstein goes the credit of developing into a more systematic conception what was isolated intuition in Saussure, and hesitating recognition in Croce's last writings.

NOTES

[1] "Il faut avouer qu'il y a là (dans le jugement d'identité ou de non identité) un élément subjectif, mai commun à toutes les personnes. Cependant il est très difficile de voir où il y a identité. Et nos identités sont la base. Tout le mécanisme de la langue roule autour d'identités et de différences."

[2] "Quello che si chiama lingua fuori della produzione, della contemplazione e del giudizio di espressività, la lingua dei linguisti [...] dev'essere [...] tutt'altra cosa, rientrante nella vita morale dell'uomo, tra le sue appetizioni, i suoi desideri, le sue volizioni e azioni, le sue abitudini, i voli della sua immaginazione, le mode del suo comportamento (e tra esse anche la moda di attribuire uno o altro significato ai suoni articolati o di pronunciarli in un modo o in un altro), in tutto ciò che per sè è un fare pratico."

[3] "Che cosa sono i singoli vocaboli, oggetto di tali investigazioni? Ho proposto e ri-propongo di chiamarli 'segni': segni fonici, mimici, grafici o combinati tra loro, o come altro si esaminino e si classifichino. E che è il segno? [...] La volontà ed azione pratica, per quelle ragioni di vita che si dicono di comunicazione sociale (e qui non bisogna dimenticare d'includere nella società la società con noi stessi e la comunicazione a noi stessi, entro di noi), interviene a fissare ed elaborare questi svariati sintomi, innal-zandoli con la sua elaborazione a segni [...] come espedienti e mezzi pratici per richia-mare le cose o i fatti e, come dire?, per designarli."

CHAPTER VII

THE *PHILOSOPHICAL INVESTIGATIONS* AND THE RISE OF A NEW SEMANTICS

It has been said that the *Philosophical Investigations* may be thought of as a book of pure philosophy of language. This is largely true. If, however, we are to understand this book we must remember that, as Wittgenstein himself states in the Introduction (p. X), it is the *Tractatus* turned upside down. It should be understood as such. This means that in it there are *also* a methodology and an ontology entirely different from that of the *Tractatus*. And if the *Tractatus* cannot be entirely understood without taking into account the rôle played in it by ideas about language, the *Investigations* cannot be understood without considering the methodology and ontology accompanying the ideas about language developed in it.

The nucleus of the methodology of the *Investigations* may be found in this paragraph:

> "We feel as if we had to penetrate phenomena: our investigation, however, is directed not towards phenomena, but, as one might say, toward the 'possibilities' of phenomena. We remind ourselves, that is to say, of the *kind of statement* that we make about phenomena" (90).

Wittgenstein is not concerned, therefore, to discover phenomena, let alone, therefore, to show that certain phenomena exist. He attempts to make clear the conditions in which we know phenomena, that is the modalities of our statements about them.

> "The [*philosophical*] problems are solved, not by giving new information, but by arranging what we have always known." (109)

> "Philosophy simply puts everything before us, and neither explains nor deduces anything. – Since everything lies open to view there is nothing to explain […]. One might also give the name 'philosophy' to what is possible *before* all new discoveries and inventions." (126)

> "The work of the philosopher consists in assembling reminders for a particular purpose." (127)

(Here Wittgenstein not only sides with, but puts himself in the vanguard of, the "modern gnoseology" of which LOMBARDI, 1963, p. 181 speaks.)

This methodology of philosophical enquiry, as the clarification of possibilities, or of kinds of statements, is correlated to a particular conception of human knowledge.

That there are primary elements in reality has been maintained by a long tradition, from the *Theaetetus* of Plato up to Russell and to the early Wittgenstein himself. These primary elements (Russell's 'individuals', Wittgenstein's 'objects') are the simple constituent parts of which reality is composed. This point of view is of great inportance for linguistics. As we noted earlier, the conception of language as a nomenclature relies on the acceptance of this traditional point of view, as do the so-called 'modern' semantic theories like the 'semantic triangle' of OGDEN and RICHARDS (1923, p. 11), modified in its details by ULLMANN's (1951, p. 71ff; 1962, p. 55), and the behaviouristic theories of Morris. The great European philosophers of the seventeenth and eighteenth centuries and modern linguists like Saussure and Martinet have criticized this conception listing the 'deplacements', the shifts, and the 'entorses', the distortions, in the parallelism between series of meanings in the various languages. Series of meanings in any language are incommensurable with those in any other: this proves that no series of meanings can be considered as based, in the end, on the designation of a universal and eternal series of concepts and/ or categories of things. Despite himself, the early Wittgenstein suggests an internal criticism of the idea of language as nomenclature. The later Wittgenstein strikes at the very heart of this conception: he argues that we cannot speak of 'primary elements' or of 'simple elements' in any absolute sense.

He writes (47):

"But what are the simple constituent parts of which reality is composed? What are the simple constituent parts of a chair? – The bits of wood of which it is made? Or the molecules, or the atoms? – 'Simple' means: not composite. And here the point is: in what sense 'composite'? It makes no sense at all to speak absolutely of the 'simple parts of a chair'.

Again: Does my visual image of this tree, of this chair, consist of parts? And what are its simple component parts? Multi-colouredness is one kind of complexity; another is, for example, that of a broken outline composed of straight bits. And a curve can be said to be composed of an ascending and descending segment.

If I tell someone without any further explanation: 'What I see before me now is composite', he will have the right to ask: 'What do you mean by *composite*? For there are all sorts of things that that can mean!' – The question 'Is what you see composite?' makes good sense if it is already established what kind of complexity – that is, which particular use of the word –

is in question. If it had been laid down that the visual image of a tree was to be called 'composite' if one saw not just a single trunk, but also branches, then the question 'Is the visual image of this tree simple or composite?', and the question 'What are its simple component parts?', would have a clear sense – a clear use.

But isn't a chessboard, for instance, obviously, and absolutely, composite? – You are probably thinking of the composition out of thirty-two white and thirty-two black squares. But could we not also say, for instance, that it was composed of the colours black and white and the schema of squares? And if there are quite different ways of looking at it, do you still want to say that the chessboard is absolutely 'composite'? – Asking 'Is the object composite?' outside a particular language-game is like what a boy once did, who had to say whether the verbs in certain sentences were in the active or passive voice, and who racked his brains over the question whether the verb 'to sleep' meant something active or passive.

We use the word 'composite' (and therefore the word 'simple') in an enormous number of different and differently related ways. (Is the colour of a square on a chessboard simple, or does it consist of pure white and pure yellow? And is white simple, or does it consist of the colours of the rainbow? – Is this length of 2 cm. simple or does it consist of two parts, each 1 cm. long? But why not of one bit 3 cm. long, and one bit 1 cm. long measured in the opposite direction?)"

Thus, to summarize, the simplicity or complexity of an object depends on the co-ordinates in relation to which the object is considered. The simple or composite object is not a datum pre-existing to the choice of co-ordinates and hence to the experience of man. Or, Wittgenstein in the *Investigations* demonstrates the falsehood of the "simplicistic idea that the whole world is ordered, before man's vision of it, in perfectly distinct categories of objects", the same idea discussed and rejected by MARTINET (1960, p. 15). Language intervenes to determine the choice of the co-ordinates according to which we build simple and/or composite objects. As Wittgenstein shows, it intervenes in two ways. It intervenes meta-linguistically: when we judge an object's simplicity or complexity we have first to define the words *simple* and *composite*.

"To the philosophical question: 'Is the visual image of this tree composite, and what are its component parts?' the correct answer is: 'That depends on what you understand by 'composite'." (47)

But language more commonly intervenes in another way, not at the level of judgement on the meaning of 'simplicity' and 'complexity' but at the level of the immediate construction of categories of objects. The possession of a word is in fact, if not the unique, at least one of the most

45

common landmarks used by individuals and communities to distinguish not only notions without a sensorial reference, that is 'abstract ideas' (OGDEN and RICHARDS, 1923, pp. 40–47; PAGLIARO, 1952, p. 26ff), but also every other category of acts and objects, as indeed became clear to experimental psychology at the end of the nineteenth century (PAGLIARO, 1952, p. 238ff; WHORF, 1958, pp. 50–56, 109, 213–14; VYGOTSKY, 1962, p. 52ff, 153; MOUNIN, 1963, p. 24ff).

On these arguments Cassirer's *Philosophie der symbolischen Formen* has basic importance (see especially CASSIRER, 1954, vol. III, p. 20ff). This function of words did not escape Wittgenstein's attention. See *Investigations* §§ 65–75 on the reasons allowing us to speak of 'games', 'numbers' or 'leaves' as kindred classes or entities, notwithstanding differences. In the end we must conclude from these paragraphs that at the roots of these three classes, as at those of others, there is an affinity between different objects, one which is revealed by words. This interpretation is confirmed by 381 and 384: "How do I know that this colour is red? – It would be an answer to say: 'I have learnt English'"; "You learned the concept 'pain' when you learned language". But above all from 371 and 373: "*Essence* is expressed by grammar"; "Grammar tells what kind of object anything is. (Theology as grammar.)".

A first consequence concerning the method of semantic analysis arises from these considerations. It is not correct to describe the meaning of a word by starting from the thing or concept it is assumed to designate. Semantic analysis must first of all start from the use of the word. Wittgenstein puts this aptly (43):

"For a large class of cases, though not for all, in which we employ the word 'meaning' it can be defined thus: the meaning of a word is its use in the language."

It is to be noted that the ostensive definition thus becomes not the rule, but a limiting case among the possible descriptions of meaning: "And the *meaning* of a name is sometimes explained by pointing to its *bearer*" (43; see also 2). The fact that Wittgenstein admits the limiting possibility of ostensive definitions immediately proves that his interpretation of meaning as *use* does not coincide with that of meaning as mere "legality" in the use of a form, without any extralinguistic correlation. Wittgenstein does not consider speech as a mere phonic game, regulated by certain curious and complicated laws, but the production of propositions correlated to extralinguistic data and behaviour. It is therefore to be described in

46

conformity with them and not as the mere production of insignificant forms.

When Wittgenstein maintains that what is generally called *meaning* (or, in other European languages, *signifié, significato, Bedeutung*) coincides with use he does not mean to reduce semantics to the mere sum of morphemic and syntagmatic-distributional descriptions. He seeks to transform semantics from the science of meaning or meanings (the traditional conception reflected even in the current definitions of semantics in the various European languages, and in German in the very name of *Bedeutungslehre*: see READ, 1948) into the science of the signifying activity. He rejects the traditional idea of linguistic forms and their meanings as classes of entities which are co-related in themselves, either by the identity of the human spirit, or by reason of the system (the conception whose difficulties and drawbacks we have already discussed). He seeks to impose a new vision in which linguistic forms have the meaning they do because they are used by man, the guarantee of their validity being found only in their use. From being the science of the *sēmainómena* semantics thus becomes the science of the *sēmaínein*.

As may be seen, Wittgenstein's thought is here very close to Saussure's isolated idea and to the thought of the later Croce. They have in common the idea that meaning is dependent on signifying activity (and not vice-versa) and that, more generally, language (the *langue* in Saussurian terminology) depends on speaking activity (the *parler*). Linguistic behaviour, not linguistic forms or meanings, is thus at the root of linguistic and semantic descriptions. This idea is now often to be found in very different terms and cultural settings. It has equally influenced a philosopher with an idealistic background (CALOGERO, 1947, pp. 124-45, 181, 194-95; CALOGERO et al., 1958, pp. 58-66), a linguist concerned with the problems of learning (SIERTSEMA, 1961), and a traditional comparative philologist (PISANI, 1959, pp. 1-28). The idea that "il simbolo fonico vive della vita dei parlanti", "the phonic symbol lives by the life of its speakers" (PAGLIARO, 1952, p. 61) and does not transmit values and meaning except by its use, is as vigorously present in all of them. "Every sign by *itself* seems dead. *What* gives it life? – In use it is *alive*" (432).

Wittgenstein does not confine himself to upholding the thesis of meaning as use. He also clarifies it, safeguarding it from possible objections. The thesis may have two interpretations, according to our conception of use. In any event it is clear that use is use by individuals. But we can conceive this use in an individualistic sense. Use is sometimes interpreted by Calogero in this way. Rightly concerned that the reference to language should lead again to metaphysical and Platonic positions, CALOGERO (1947, pp. 194–95) writes:

"Every Plato who asks 'what is virtue?' finds a Socrates to remind him of the need for exactness, enquiring 'What do you mean by *virtue*? [...] What do you really mean when you speak of virtue?' The criticism of concepts is in fact never anything else but this Socratic 'inquiry into discourse', continuously asking the speaker to make the meaning of his words clearer [...]. The only really important thing [...] is to understand what Tom, Dick and Harry in fact mean when they use those terms, what sum of direct experience and aspirations they seek to present by the repetition of those schemata."[1]

Calogero seems to establish an alternative without other possibilities. Either we admit that words have a meaning in themselves (thus going back to a Platonic, Aristotelian and rationalistic conception of language with all the objections to which, as we have said, it gives rise); or we admit that the meaning of a word depends exclusively on its use by the individual, who treats it absolutely freely, only limited by "the well-known social precept that it is not legitimate to alter the meaning of a term too much, because listeners' habits have their rights too" (CALOGERO, 1947, p. 195). Calogero, therefore, does not deny that words can have the same meaning when uttered by different people. But he explains this coincidence as the result of good manners, of the courtesy of the speaker. Just as people walking along the street try not to bump into each other, so they try not to use words too differently when they speak. But, just as the fact that well-mannered people try not to bump into each other need not be taken into account in a scientific description of the motor processes of the human body, similarly the fact that people try to use words in the same way need not concern us in describing linguistic processes. Compared with the fact that a person uses a word, the fact that he uses it in the same way as other people is secondary.

Various kinds of objections can be raised to this individualistic conception of use. It is, above all, a bad description of real linguistic behaviour. If the only guarantee of the meaning of a word was really set in its use by an individual, the listener would have to keep on asking "What do you mean by...?". This does not usually happen. But suppose for a moment that it did. The other could and must in turn legitimately ask: "What do you mean by 'what do you mean?'?". In the end, dialogue, as Calogero sees it, could become an endless re-echoing of questions like "What do you mean by 'what'?" or, still more exactly, "What?". The individualistic conception of the use of words not only badly describes what happens when we speak, but, if speech were as the individualists conceive it, no communication would be possible.

Must we think of words as in themselves endowed with meaning if we want to avoid these objections? Is there no way of avoiding the objections we can make to Socrates – or to a sophist – but that of seeing language like Plato – and Aristotle? (In fact it may be noted that, historically, it is not Socrates who reminds Plato of "the need for exactness"; on the contrary, Plato's – and above all Aristotle's – conception of language springs from the need to build a barrier against the individualistic conception of language use put forward by Socrates and sophists. We have already briefly discussed the beginning of this historical process, to which we shall return elsewhere.) As a matter of fact, Calogero suggests a third possibility elsewhere in his book (p. 181):

"The truth is that the sign is connected to meaning by the historical tradition gradually created and evolved by the endless repetition and renewal of human speech, and the historical tradition must be respected because it is as difficult as it is unwarranted to do otherwise [...]. From this point of view, nothing is more purely instrumental, more entirely subordinated to the possibilities of its use, than is language. Its virtue lies entirely in its efficiency as a means of communication: if we thereby understand each other, its purpose is fulfilled [...]. Hence use – that is the most frequent and established habits of speakers – is the ultimate rule of functional correctness of a language." [2]

The meaning of a word, therefore, does not depend on its use by an individual *uti singulus*, but, Calogero hints, on its use by an individual who belongs to a certain historical community and is therefore forced to avoid arbitrary and purely personal whims in using words.

In the *Philosophical Investigations* this point of view is amply developed and combined with the other according to which the meaning of a word is protected from individual whims not only by the social training to which the individual is submitted but also by the fact that a word is one of a complex body of signs whose parts cannot be changed from one moment to another *ad libitum*.

The first paragraphs of the *Investigations* in fact develop the first of these two points of view. Even in "a language more primitive than ours" (2), whose lexemes are closely associated to determine categories of objects, without training in the setting of a particular community and unless individuals are organized in society, the meaningful use of lexemes is impossible. Even very simple lexical elements are empty or equivocal outside the context of a certain training and social organization (see also DEWEY, 1938, pp. 36–47, 53). Even in this case the ostensive teaching of lexemes may be useful and initially indispensable, but it is not enough to guarantee the effective use of the lexeme:

"But if the ostensive teaching has this effect, – am I to say that it effects an understanding of the word? Don't you understand the call 'Slab!' if you act upon it in such-and-such a way? – Doubtless the ostensive teaching helped to bring this about; but only together with a particular training. With different training the same ostensive teaching of these words would have effected a quite different understanding.

'I set the brake up by connecting up rod and lever'. – Yes, given all the rest of the mechanism. Only in conjunction with that it is a brake-lever, and separated from its support it is not even a lever; it may be anything or nothing." (6)

Analysing possible examples of linguistic games Wittgenstein arrives at the conclusion which Nida and Mounin reach by a different route: the meaning and value of every linguistic sign is embodied in the "ethnography" of the society in which it is adopted (DEWEY, 1938, p. 50; NIDA, 1945; MOUNIN, 1963, pp. 227–41). This bond with "all the rest of the mechanism" of a society (and perhaps of a language: Wittgenstein's thought in this passage is uncertain) is the first factor keeping the sign clear from individual whim. Here Wittgenstein can say:

It is easy to imagine a language consisting only of orders and reports in battle. Or a language consisting only of questions and expressions for answering yes and no. And innumerable others. — And to imagine a language means to imagine a form of life." (19)

But there is a second factor, no less important in Wittgenstein's eyes: the systematic factor. For a linguist formed in the historical and/or structural school, used to accepting the idea of a linguistic system somewhat dogmatically, there always exists the theoretical and perhaps also psychological possibility of being assailed by doubts in this regard. It is really true that not only linguistic behaviour, acts of *parole*, i.e. acts of speech, exists but also the *langue*, the linguistic system? Is not the description of linguistic facts without considering the linguistic system a program thriving on a very different cultural soil? Is there not substantial agreement between the early Croce or an historical linguist like Pisani, who believes that the linguistic systems are a "mythologeme" (PISANI, 1959, p. 11ff; see also TERRACINI, 1963, *passim*), and the conception supported by the semiotics of Morris, who considers linguistic signs under three aspects, the pragmatic, the semantic and the syntactic, and ignores the existence of a fourth "systematic" dimension?

Wittgenstein offers a very useful antidote to these doubts. He did not of course inherit the notion of a "system" from the tradition of his studies but, we may say, built it up from the analysis of the linguistic behaviour of individuals.

> But now it looks as if when someone says 'Bring me a slab!' he could mean this expression as *one* long word corresponding to the single word 'slab!' – Then can one mean it sometimes as one word and sometimes as four? And how does one usually mean it? — I think we shall be inclined to say: we mean the sentence as *four* words when we use it in contrast with other sentences as '*Hand* me a slab', 'Bring *him* a slab', 'Bring *two* slabs', etc.; that is, in contrast with sentences containing the separate words of our command in other combinations. — But what does using one sentence in contrast with others consist in? Do the others, perhaps, hover before one's mind? *All* of them? [*We may note here that Saussure replies affirmatively to this question, and that his affirmative reply is the main source of the difficulties of his theory*.] And *while* one is saying the one sentence, or before, or afterwards? – No. Even if such an explanation rather tempts us, we need only think for a moment of what actually happens in order to see that we are going astray here. We say that we use the command in contrast with other sentences because *our language* contains the possibility of those other sentences. Someone who did not understand our language, a foreigner, who had fairly often heard someone giving the order: 'Bring me a slab!', might believe that this whole series of sounds was one word corresponding perhaps to the word for 'building-stone' in his language." (20)

The use of a linguistic sign is thus related to all the possibilities of the use of other linguistic signs. The very possibility of being identified (and therefore used by the speaker and the listener) depends on the possibility of being replaced by other signs. We again stress some coincidences. Firstly, in terms of the Italian tradition, we may say that a language is an 'institution' as the later Croce and sometimes Calogero suggest, and NENCIONI (1946) and DEVOTO (1951, p. 6ff) believe. But not as if it consisted of a body of rules of which each could apply independently of the others (BOBBIO, 1958, pp. 3–13). The institution of language is a body of co-functional parts and rules, which are cogent and exist as co-functional: that is, the language is the technique of speech, as PAGLIARO, 1952, 1957, believes. Moreover, Wittgenstein's idea corresponds exactly to basic concepts of John Dewey's *Logic*:

"I turn now to the positive implication of the fact that no sound, mark, product of art, is a word or part of a language in isolation. Any word or phrase has the meaning which it has only as a member of a constellation of related meanings. Words as representatives are part of an inclusive code [...] In every case, a particular word has its meaning only in relation to the code of which it is one constituent." (DEWEY, 1938, p. 49; see also HOCKETT, 1958, p. 15)

This point of view may be re-formulated in technical terms by saying that the need for paradigmatic differentiation, and hence the linguistic system, is based on the need to distinguish – in the most economical way – the greatest number of different structures (in the sense of "sequences of linguistic units") in relation to the need of communicating various meanings. As meaning depends on the use of socially-organized individuals, so the system of different forms necessary to indicate the various meanings by their alternations and combinations is based upon the structure of the proposition, and more precisely on the necessity of building such structures economically. Theoretically, different structures could be built with different unities, each of which would be employed in one structure and in one only. In this way every structure would be entirely – in all elements composing it – different from every other. This would certainly give the maximum of individuality to each structure, to each proposition, and hence the maximum adherence to the situation to be communicated. There would be no such things as a structure, since there would be no alternative forms in the same place within the structure, but there would be only the sum of structures and phrases. (So an artistic "language", the "language" of architecture or of music is the mere sum of single artistic pieces.) The early Croce thought that language functioned in this way. It has already been stated that, if this were so, language would not satisfy the need of establishing a certain meaningful content for oneself and others. We may add that of course the burden on the memory of man would be far greater than it could bear. "What is your aim in philosophy? – To shew the fly the way out of the fly-bottle" (309). Like every good work of philosophy, the *Philosophical Investigations* help our thought to escape from the dilemma between the conception of linguistic facts put forward by Plato and Aristotle, by Descartes and the early Wittgenstein, by the early Croce and Saussure (that is: linguistic forms have a certain meaning in themselves, because they represent things or concepts which are equal for everybody, or because they are connected in a system, or on account of the perfect identity between individual states of mind and individual expressions) and the individualistic conception (that is: these linguistic forms have this meaning because I give – or you give – them this meaning).

It is clear that language, as conceived by Wittgenstein, does not presuppose a complete knowledge of things and facts. On the contrary, as we have seen, its elements, its lexemes and patterns help the member of a certain community to distinguish certain relationships between the single things, and therefore, to build a first nucleus of knowledge around them. This releases the conception of language from the difficulties observed by Vico (one need not have "sat at the feet of Aristotle" nor have taken academic degrees in order to speak) and from the absurd conclusions of the *Tractatus* (given that the formulation and understanding of a proposition presuppose a complete knowledge of facts and things, speech is completely useless because nothing can be communicated unless it is already known). This conception of language, moreover, describes a language not as a completely inter-dependent system ("un système tout serré"), but rather as an open system, a "systematization". A proposition is scarcely usable without this systematization, without the reference to a language having alternative possibilities, but it is not necessary to know all these possibilities to use a proposition. Certainly, this means that our use of speech will be more or less precise, as will be our reaction to a proposition, according to the greater or lesser number of alternatives to the proposition or its parts available to us. This is precisely what commonly happens. But if we describe language as an open system we are able to explain why there is always a minimal degree of communication. It is not necessary to assume, with Saussure, that a linguistic system does not change through time, or with social classes or individuals, to allow the possibility of mutual understanding between social classes, people of different linguistic capacities and historical periods.

Wittgenstein also recognizes the rôle played in human speech by the training of a given society and the reference to common possibilities of building linguistic signs. This rescues his description from the objections which, as we have seen, may be made about the individualistic conception of linguistic behaviour. Of course, it is you who, speaking to me, give a certain meaning to the propositions you use and to the words composing them. But in the measure in which you belong to my own community, you have been subjected to a linguistic and cultural training similar to my own and I have valid grounds for supposing that your propositions have a similar meaning for both of us. And the 'hypothesis' which I make when I

53

hear you speak, and which you make speaking to me, is confirmed for both of us by both your and my total behaviour.

The locutions 'more or less', 'similar', 'valid grounds for supposing' are distressingly common in the above paragraphs for those who are used to the 'yes' and 'no', to the absolute affirmations and negations of a large part of traditional philosophy. Guido Calogero has gathered many objections to this "Manichaean logic" of 'yes' and 'no'. The later Wittgenstein also explicitly rejects it (which perhaps constitutes the most profound difference between the early and the later Wittgenstein). The general question, however, does not concern us here. Abstractly there is perhaps a domain of thought in which only absolute certainty or absolute rejection is possible. But, on the basis of the later thought of Wittgenstein, perfect communication, or total lack of communication, can be thought of only as limits never reached by speaker and hearer and between which they move. In fact the strength of linguistic and semantic scepsis lies entirely in the belief that communication does, or does not, exist, that a proposition is perfectly understood or is not understood at all, perfectly translated or untranslatable. Man saves himself from the whirlpool of incommunicability only by landing on the Fortunate Isle of Perfect Understanding. Kierkegaard thought of this island as God. In fact, in the world of men there are infinite shades between perfect communication and the entire lack of communication. There are found to be universals, cosmological and biological, allowing a minimum of contact and understanding (by natural training) even between people of entirely different language-types (MOUNIN, 1963, pp. 213–23). And even the most experienced philologist knows the sudden 'dizziness' (the late Leo Spitzer called it a sudden 'click') which comes over him when he discovers a richer, more precise meaning for a proposition already read a hundred times.

Wittgenstein's final conclusion seems to be just this. Linguistic behaviour is always more or less successful. Other scholars have reached the same conclusions from different starting points. Thus MOUNIN (1963, pp. 178–79) writes:

"When I say, quoting Mallarmé, *La chair est triste, hélas!, et j'ai lu tous les livres*, my listener can understand this statement: (a) at the lowest level of social communication (The listener, a bright fourth-form boy, understands the vocabulary and the syntax of the proposition. He almost certainly asks himself how one can say that the flesh is sad; and if one can really say that one has read all the books); (b) at the level, close to that of the first, of the elaboration of thought (The bright fifth-former understands that "the flesh is sad" represents the poet's judgement on life and the pleasures of the flesh as opposed to those of the spirit; he also understands that "I have read all the books" is a hyperbole); (c) at the level of the function of affective values (The gifted sixth-form student knows something about the life of Mallarmé and his ideas, notably about his quasi-deification of books. He also grasps the cultural overtones – literary, religious, philosophical and moral – of the word *chair* in French); (d) at the level of the aesthetic function of language. The same boy would perhaps feel the solidity of the verse line, the balance of its antithesis, its phonic values, the weight that can be given to it in speech [...]. These levels, separate in analysis, can of course be intermingled, very differently, by the same speaker." [3]

And PAGLIARO (1952, p. 310) observes:

"In general it may be said that a linguistic system is able to convey, in the semantic value of a sign, only an incredibly small number of the cognitive potentialities of the mind and of the unnumerable and varied moments of our affective life. It is true that the generic nature of signs and the infinity of their combinations – which best determine meaning – are the greatest help to those who can take advantage of them; all the same, the fullness of reality [...] is substantially incommunicable. It is such that the linguistic sign is only a reminder, an allusion [...]. Considering it soberly, the symbol shows itself in the end to be an expedient, no matter how brilliant, but still an expedient." [4]

The recognition of the 'expedient' nature of the proposition and of its unities (and hence of language) is very important. It is the basis on which semantics may be built.

On the basis of the individualistic conception of linguistic facts, semantics is only possible as an indefinite series of analysis of innumerable particular situations; Calogero rightly drew this conclusion from the premise, going so far as to write that any other semantic analysis (always in the setting of the individualistic premises) would be only "idle chat" ("chiacchiera"). No discipline can be built up on an individualistic basis; only a large number of judgements on particular situations can be made.

On the basis of Platonic-Aristotelian and rationalistic premises, semantics naturally coincides with the knowledge of all the possible contents of every linguistic act. This has been aptly noted by BLOOMFIELD (pp. 138–39) who considers that the construction of semantics would imply the acquisition of a scientific kind of knowledge of every nameable thing. Now,

we can define the names of minerals, for example, in terms of chemistry and mineralogy..., but we have no precise way of defining words like *love* or *hate*, which concern situations that have not been accurately classified – and these latter are in the great majority.

This makes the project of the construction of semantics effectively impracticable and explains Bloomfield's doubt on the subject.

We have attempted to show how the work of other scholars, from Cassirer to Pagliaro and Martinet, tends towards the central and final conclusions of Wittgenstein's conception of language: it is indeed a good foundation for the construction of a semantics that is neither an infinite series of single observations nor the *scientia de omnibus rebus et de nonnullis aliis*. There is therefore a place, and a fairly clearly defined one, for the descriptive (i.e. both synchronic and diachronic) study and for the interpretative study of a class of phenomena. This class is made up of the ways in which the *sēmaínein*, the signifying activity of men, is realized at the levels of common speech of different human communities. These ways, as we have seen, are not completely variable from one person to another and therefore they are a legitimate subject for statements with a generalized content. And, since they are not necessarily all simultaneously present in the speaker or listener, as Wittgenstein has rightly shown, it is not necessary to account for all of them even in heuristic and descriptive discussions. Semantics can thus be constructed within the limits of human possibilities, that is, of the actual ones, and not within those of an omniscient and utopian humanity.

"Philosophy assembles reminders for a particular purpose" (127). And a purpose, in the case of the *Philosophical Investigations*, is the construction of semantics as the science of signifying activity. Wittgenstein's thought can perhaps lead to other goals. Other readings of his work are possible: the present attempt does not claim to be the only one. A late-classical writer once justified the many and very different interpretations of Homer by the presence in Homer, as in every classic author, of a *palíntropos harmonía*. He wanted to say that Homer and the classic authors resound with various echoes to various readers. And Wittgenstein is doubtless a classic.

NOTES

1 "Di fronte a ogni Platone che domandi: – Che cosa è la virtù? –, torna sempre a sorgere un Socrate che lo richiama all'esattezza chiedendo: – Che cosa intendi per 'virtù'?... Che cosa propriamente intendi significare, quando parli di 'virtù'? – La reale critica dei concetti non è mai altro che questo socratico 'inquisire il discorso', domandando senza

tregua all'interlocutore di precisare sempre meglio il significato delle sue parole [...]. La sola cosa che [...] veramente importa è quella di capire che cosa [...] Caio, Tizio e Sempronio intendano in concreto quando adoperano quei termini, quale somma di dirette esperienze e aspirazioni di vita mirino a far presente con la ripetizione di quegli schemi".

[2] "La realtà è che il segno è connesso al significato dalla tradizione storica venutasi lentamente costituendo ed evolvendo attraverso l'infinito ripetersi e rinnovarsi del colloquio umano, e che conviene sempre rispettare anche in ogni parziale innovazione, perchè fare altrimenti significherebbe affrontare un'impresa tanto difficile quanto gratuita [...]. Per questo aspetto, nulla di più strumentale, di più radicalmente subordinato alle sua capacità d'uso, del linguaggio. La sua bontà è tutta nella sua efficienza comunicativa: se con esso ci si intende, lo scopo è raggiunto. Di qui il fatto che nell'uso, cioè nella più frequente o stabilizzata consuetudine dei parlanti, sia il canone ultimo della funzionale correttezza d'una lingua".

[3] "Quand je dis, citant Mallarmé, *La chair est triste, hélas!, et j'ai lu tous les livres* mon auditeur peut saisir cet énoncé: a) soit au niveau de la fonction de communication sociale minimum (l'auditeur, un enfant doué du cours moyen deuxième anné, comprend le vocabulaire et la syntaxe de la phrase. Il se demande presque sûrement pourquoi l'on peut dire que la chair est triste; et si quelq'un peut vraiment dire qu'il a lu tous les livres); b) soit au niveau, tout proche du premier, de la fonction d'élaboration de la pensée (l'auditeur, un élève moyen de la classe troisième, comprend que *la chair est triste* est un jugement du poète sur la vie et les plaisirs de la chair, opposée à l'esprit; il comprend aussssi que *j'ai lu tous les livres* est une expression hyperbolique); c) soit au niveau de la fonction des valeurs affectives (l'auditeur, un élève doué de seconde ou de première, sait quelque chose de la vie de Mallarmé, de ses idées, notamment sa quasi-déification du Livre. Il connaît aussi les connotations culturelles en français, bibliques, religieuses, philosophiques, morales, du mot *chair* [...]); d) soit au niveau de la fonction esthétique du langage. Le même élève doué saisit peut-être [...] la solidité du vers, son équilibre dans l'antithèse, ses valeurs phoniques, la pesanteur qu'on peut donner à sa diction [...]. Naturellement, ces niveaux, séparés par l'analyse, peuvent eux-mêmes s'entremêler, avec des valeurs très divers, chez le même locuteur [...]."

[4] "In generale può dirsi che nelle possibilità conoscitive della mente e dei momenti innumeri e variabilissimi della nostra vita affettiva, quelli che un sistema linguistico riesce a fissare nel valore semantico del segno sono di numero incredibilmente limitato. È vero che la genericità del segno e le infinite combinazioni dei nessi, nei quali il significato si determina, forniscono un grandissimo aiuto a chi sa giovarsene; ma con tutto ciò la realtà nella sua pienezza [...] è sostanzialmente incomunicabile. Egli è che il segno linguistico è soltanto un richiamo, un'allusione [...]. A considerarlo pacatamente, il simbolo alla fine rivela la sua natura di espediente, ingegnoso per quanto si voglia. ma sempre espediente."

REFERENCES

ANSCOMBE, G. E. M. (1959), *An Introduction to Wittgenstein's Tractatus*, London.

APEL, K. O. (1963), 'Die Idee der Sprache in der Tradition des Humanismus von Dante bis Vico', *Archiv für Begriffsgeschichte*, Vol. VIII.

ARENS, H. (1955), *Sprachwissenschaft. Der Gang ihrer Entwicklung von der Antike bis zur Gegenwart*, München.

BACON, Francis (1665), *Opera omnia*, Frankfurt, coll. 144–47.

BARONE, F. (1953), *Il neopositivismo logico*, Torino.

BELARDI, W. (1959), *Elementi di fonologia generale*, Roma.

BLOCH, B. (1948), 'A Set of Postulates for Phonemic Analysis', *Language* **24**, 3–46.

BLOOMFIELD, L. (1933), *Language*, New York.

BOBBIO, N. (1958), *Teoria della norma giuridica*, Torino.

BOLELLI, T. (1965), *Per una storia della ricerca linguistica*, Napoli.

BRÉAL, M. (1866), 'Introduction', in BOPP, F., *Grammaire comparée des langues indo-européennes...* (trad. M. Bréal), Vol. I, Paris.

CALOGERO, G. (1947), *Estetica, semantica, istorica*, Torino.

CALOGERO, G., DE MAURO, T., and SASSO, G. (1958), 'Intorno alla storia del significato di 'democrazia' in Italia', *Il ponte* **14**, 39–66.

CARNAP, R. (1928), *Der logische Aufbau der Welt*, Berlin.

CASSIRER, E. (1954), *Philosophie der symbolischen Formen*, 2. Ed., 3 Vols, Tübingen.

CAVACIUTI, S. (1959), *La teoria linguistica di Benedetto Croce*, Milano.

CECCATO, S. (1960), 'Operational Linguistics and Translations' in *Linguistic and Programming for Mechanical Translation*, Milano, pp. 11–80.

COLOMBO, G. C. M. (1954), 'Introduzione critica' in *L. W. Tractatus Logico-philosophicus. Testo originale, versione italiana a fronte*, Milano, pp. 11–131.

COSERIU, E. (1962), *Teoría del lenguaje y lingüística general*, Madrid.

CROCE, B. (1899–1900), *Di alcuni principî di sintassi e stilistica psicologica del Gröber*, 1899; *Le categorie rettoriche e il professor Gröber*, 1900. Cf. CROCE (1910, pp. 141–52, 153–59).

CROCE, B. (1902), *Estetica come scienza dell'espressione e linguistica generale*, 1. Ed., Palermo, 1902, 8. Ed., Bari, 1945.

CROCE, B. (1908), *Logica come scienza del concetto puro*, 1. Ed., Bari, 1908, 7. Ed., *ibid.*, 1954.

CROCE, B. (1910), *Problemi di estetica*, 1. Ed., Bari, 1910, 5. Ed., *ibid.*, 1954.

CROCE, B. (1935), *La poesia. Introduzione alla critica e storia della letteratura e della poesia*, Bari.

CROCE, B. (1941), 'La filosofia del linguaggio e le sue condizioni presenti in Italia', in *Discorsi di varia filosofia*, Vol. I, Bari, 1945, pp. 235–50.

CROCE, B. (1950), 'Sulla natura e l'ufficio della linguistica', in *Letture di poeti*, Bari, pp. 247–53.

CROCE, B. (1951), *Carteggio Croce–Vossler 1899–1949*, Bari.

DE MAURO, T. (1954), 'Origine e sviluppo della linguistica crociana', *Giornale critico di storia della filosofia italiana*, p. 376–91.

DE MAURO, T. (1959), 'Accusativo, transitivo, intransitivo', *Rendiconti Accademia dei Lincei*, Cl. sc. mor. s. VIII, 16, 238–58.

DE MAURO, T. (1964), 'Recenti studi sulla linguistica crociana', *De homine* 11–12, 180ff.

DEVOTO, G. (1951), *I fondamenti della storia linguistica*, Firenze.

DEVOTO, G. (1953), 'Croce storico e Croce linguista', in *Benedetto Croce* (ed. F. Flora), Milano, pp. 183–93.

DEWEY, J. (1938), *Logic. The Theory of Inquiry*, New York.

FREI, H. (1954), 'Critères de délimitation', *Word* 10, 136–45.

GLINTZ, H. (1947), *Geschichte und Kritik der Lehre von den Satzgliedern in der deutschen Grammatik*, Bern.

GODEL, R. (1957), *Les sources manuscrites du Cours de linguistique générale*, Genève-Paris.

GUYÉNOT, E. (1957), *Les sciences de la vie au XVIIe et XVIIIe siècles. L'idée d'évolution*, Paris.

HALL JR, R. A. (1950), 'La linguistica americana dal 1925 al 1950', *Ricerche linguistiche* 1, 273–302.

HAMANN, J. G. (1955), *Sämtliche Werke* (ed. Nadler), 5 Vols, Wien, Vol. II, pp. 281–289.

HARRIS, Z. S. (1951), *Methods in Structural Linguistics*, Chicago.

HEIDEGGER, M. (1935), *Sein und Zeit*, Halle a. S.

HEIDEGGER, M. (1937), *Hölderlin und das Wesen der Dichtung*, München.

HERDAN, G. (1962), *The Calculus of Linguistic Observations*, The Hague.

HOCKETT, Ch. F. (1958), *A Course in Modern Linguistics*, New York.

HUME, D. (1739), *A Treatise of Human Nature, being an Attempt to Reduce the Experimental Method of Reasoning into Moral Subjects*, London, Vol. I, p. 38.

LEIBNIZ, G. G. (1860), *Opera philosophica* (ed. J. E. Erdmann), Berlin, pp. 296–335.

LENOBLE, R. (1957), 'Origines de la pensée scientifique moderne', in *Histoire de la science* (ed. M. Daumas), Paris, pp. 369–536.

LEPSCHY, G. (1961), 'Aspetti teorici della glottologia contemporanea', *Annali Scuola Normale Sup. di Pisa*, s. II, 30, 187–267.

LEROY, M. (1963), *Les grands courants de la linguistique moderne*, Bruxelles-Paris.

LOMBARDI, F. (1963), 'Noterelle in tema di linguaggio', *De homine* 7–8, 147–242.

LUCIDI, M. (1966), *Saggi linguistici*, Napoli.

MALCOLM, N. (1958), *Ludwig Wittgenstein. A Memoir*, with a Biographical Sketch by G. H. von WRIGHT (pp. 1–22), 1st Ed., London, 1958, 1st Ed. Oxford Paperbacks, 1962.

MANDELBROT, B. (1957), 'Linguistique statistique macroscopique', in APOSTEL, L., MANDELBROT, B., and MORF, A., *Logique, language et théorie de l'information*, Paris.

MARTINET, A. (1950), Rec. to NIDA, E., 'Morphology', *Word* 6, 84–87.

MARTINET, A. (1960). *Eléments de linguistique générale*, 1e Ed., Paris, 1960, 2e Ed., *ibid.*, 1961.

MEILLET, A. (1937), *Introduction a l'étude comparative des langues indo-européennes*, 8e Ed., Paris.

MILLER, G. A. (1951), *Language and Communication*, New York.

MOUNIN, G. (1963), *Les problèmes théoriques de la traduction*, Paris.

NENCIONI, G. (1946), *Idealismo e realismo nella scienza del linguaggio*, Firenze.

NIDA, E. A. (1945), 'Linguistics and Ethnology in Translation Problems', *Word* 1, 194–208.

OGDEN, C. K. and RICHARDS, I. A. (1923), *The Meaning of Meaning. A Study of the Influence of Language upon Thought and the Science of Symbolism*, 1st Ed., London, 1923, 10th Ed., *ibid.*, 1960.

PAGLIARO, A. (1952), *Il segno vivente*, Napoli.
PAGLIARO, A. (1957), *La parola e l'immagine*, Napoli.
PAGLIARO, A. (1961), *Altri saggi di critica semantica*, Firenze-Messina.
PISANI, V. (1959), *Saggi di linguistica storica*, Torino.
PRETI, G. (1950), *Newton*, Milano.
READ, A. W. (1948), 'An Account of the Word Semantics', *Word* 4, 78–97.
REGNÉLL, H. (1958), *Semantik. Filosofiska och språkvetenskapliga grundfrågor inom betydelseläran*, Stockholm.
ROSSI, P. (1957), *Francesco Bacone. Dalla magia alla scienza*, Bari.
ROSSI, P. (1962), *I filosofi e le macchine* (1400–1700), Milano.
ROSSI-LANDI, F. (1961), *Significato, comunicazione e parlare comune*, Padova.
SAUSSURE, F. de (1916), *Cours de linguistique générale*, 1e Ed., Paris, 1916, 2e Ed., *ibid.*, 1922.
SCARAVELLI, L. (1942), *Critica del capire*, Firenze.
SCHOLZ, H. (1962), *Storia della logica*, transl. from German by E. Melandri, Milano.
SIERTSEMA, B. (1961), 'Language Learning and Language Analysis', *Lingua* 10, 128–47.
SOMMERFELT, A. (1952), 'Tendences actuelles de la linguistique générale', *Diogène* 1, 77–84.
SPINK, J. S. (1960), *French Free-thought from Gassendi to Voltaire*, London.
TERRACINI, B. A. (1963), *Lingua libera e libertà linguistica*, Torino.
TESNIÈRE, L. (1959), *Eléments de syntaxe structurale*, Paris.
TONELLI, G. (1955), 'Kant. Dall'estetica metafisica all'estetica psico-empirica. Studi sulla genesi del criticismo (1754–1771) e sulle sue fonti', *Memorie dell'Accademia delle Scienze di Torino*, s. III, t. 3, p. II.
TONELLI, G. (1964), 'Das Wiederaufleben der deutsch-aristotelischen Terminologie bei Kant während der Entstehung der "Kritik der reinen Vernunft"', *Archiv für Begriffsgeschichte* 9, 233–242.
ULLMANN, S. (1951), *The Principles of Semantics*, 1st Ed., Glasgow-Oxford, 1951, 2nd Ed., 1957.
ULLMANN, S. (1962), *Semantics. An Introduction to the Science of Meaning*, London.
VIANO, C. A. (1960), *John Locke. Dal razionalismo all'illuminismo*, Torino.
VOSSLER, K. (1908), *Positivismo e idealismo nella scienza del linguaggio*, transl. from German by T. Gnoli, Bari 1908.
VYGOTSKY, L. S. (1962), *Thought and Language* (transl. from Russian by E. HANFMANN and G. VAKAR), New York-London.
WACKERNAGEL, J. (1953), *Kleine Schriften*, 2 Vols, Göttingen.
WEINBERG, J. R. (1950), *Introduzione al positivismo logico*, transl. from English by L. Geymonat, Torino.
WELLS, R. (1954), 'Meaning and Use', *Word* 10, 235–50 (reprinted in *Psycholinguistics. A Book of Reading* (ed. S. SAPORTA), New York, 1961, pp. 269–283).
WHORF, B. L. (1958), *Language, Thought, and Reality*, New York-London.
ZIFF, P. (1960), *Semantic Analysis*, Ithaca, N.Y.
ZIFF, P. and DE MAURO, T. (1963), 'Tra arte e linguaggio', *De homine* 7–8, 25–36.

INDEX OF NAMES

Date Due